Kieran Theivam started following began covering the game in 2011, first by blogging, before launching the UK's first podcast dedicated to the women's game in 2013. Since then, he has written for various national outlets both in the United Kingdom and United States, while acting as an expert voice for radio stations including BBC 5Live and BBC World Service. He has covered a World Cup, European Championships and Champions League Finals, while cultivating relationships with players and organisations from various parts of the globe.

Jeff Kassouf has been covering soccer – with an emphasis on advancing the women's game – since 2008. In 2009, he launched The Equalizer, still the leading website dedicated exclusively to comprehensive women's soccer coverage in North America. In four years at NBC Sports, he covered two Olympics – overseeing record-breaking livestreaming and Sports Emmy-winning digital storytelling – and spearheaded digital coverage of the Premier League in the company's first three seasons with the rights. He became the first US editor of FourFourTwo in 2016, managing the launch of the iconic brand in the US market. He played soccer competitively from early childhood through college.

The Making of the Women's World Cup

....

*Defining stories
from a sport's coming of age*

KIERAN THEIVAM AND JEFF KASSOUF

ROBINSON

ROBINSON

First published in Great Britain in 2019 by Robinson

3 5 7 9 10 8 6 4 2

A CIP catalogue record for this book
is available from the British Library.

ISBN: 978-1-47214-332-7

Typeset in Scala by Hewer Text UK Ltd, Edinburgh

Printed and bound in Great Britain by CPI Group (UK) Ltd, Croydon CR0 4YY

Papers used by Robinson are from well-managed forests and other responsible sources.

Robinson
An imprint of
Little, Brown Book Group
Carmelite House
50 Victoria Embankment
London EC4Y 0DZ

An Hachette UK Company
www.hachette.co.uk

www.littlebrown.co.uk

This book is dedicated to all those players who have taken to the field at a World Cup and created moments and memories we still talk about today, as well as those whose stories are yet to be told. It is also for those who fought so hard for higher standards when so few were in their corner.

Contents

Contents

Foreword

....

Every time I put an England shirt on, I was so proud.

To put it on in the dressing room and walk out onto the field, I'd pinch myself – I felt so privileged to represent England, especially when it came to a World Cup.

Friendly games were always different. I always gave 110 per cent, and qualification games were fun because you're trying to reach a major tournament. But that feeling when you qualify and you know you're going to a World Cup, you can't beat that excitement.

Your mentality changes, because your sole focus becomes making the squad for that tournament; everything else almost feels insignificant because you've given blood, sweat and tears to be there.

Of course, there are club matches, too. Even though I was living out my dream of playing for my team, Arsenal, in the back of my mind I knew there was a World Cup around the corner, and that is the tournament every footballer wants to play in.

It's the highest level, playing against the best players and teams in the world. You face different styles of football, different challenges, and it's an opportunity to test yourself both physically and mentally.

For me, it's the be all and end all. It was the biggest tournament and it doesn't get any higher. It's the ultimate – always has been and always will be. I felt honoured to play in two World Cups, but there will always be a tinge of sadness that I wasn't able to play in more.

I had many highlights from the two tournaments I was able to play in, and I talk about some of them in my chapter on my first

World Cup in 2007. That's the tournament that truly made me as a footballer because that was where I scored my first goals at a global competition. Players who appear at World Cups live, dream and visualise those moments. They are the pinnacle of sport, the defining moments of success.

Helping your team win, that elation and feeling you get playing on the biggest stage – I get goosebumps thinking about those experiences right now, years later. I loved playing at the 2012 London Olympics, but it's different because there are so many other sports competing for attention. The World Cup is one month of football and football only – the ultimate.

I have so many of my own memorable moments of playing at a World Cup, and I know this book goes in depth to look at some of the moments that, even today, fans of the women's game can still remember. I played against many of the countries that feature, with very mixed results and recollections.

My England team actually beat the 2011 Japan side that so memorably went on to win the World Cup months after the tragedy of the earthquake and tsunami that hit the country, killing over fifteen thousand people. We took pride in beating the team that went on to become champions. They had Homare Sawa, who was their key player, great on the ball and great vision. 'Frustrating' defined our matches against Japan, because they were so good technically with the ball at their feet. It was difficult to win possession, so you had to stay mentally ready; and we knew we had to be physical. If you got in their faces, there was always a chance you could win back the ball. But Japan are the most technical side I have ever played against in terms of ball retention. They toyed with opponents. They were a real tough game when you were involved, and a joy to watch when you were not.

Every time I played against the USA, it was about mental toughness, and I always felt they had a mental edge. I learnt and observed during my years out there in college, at Seton Hall University – and then on the two occasions I played in their professional leagues – that they have that winning desire, whether it was in training or on matchday.

They have always been at the forefront of fitness and strength, dominating games with their power and speed. They had the benefit of being in regular camps, pushing each other every day, and through that you get a strong feeling of togetherness. They haven't always been the most technical side, but when you have the speed, the strength and the mentality, that's a hard thing to come up against – and a big reason for their three World Cup titles, which are explored in this book. We didn't have that winning mentality with England, so we always found it hard against them.

Germany are the only team to date to win back-to-back World Cups in the women's game, and they, too, are just so physically dominant.

They had technical players like legendary captain Birgit Prinz. She was strong, she was powerful, she was fast and she was smart. She could dominate defences and when you have someone like that, you have a very good chance of winning games. They had technical players like Renate Lingor, Maren Meinert and Steffi Jones – big players who could dominate you. I played with and against Doris Fitschen just before Germany won their back-to-back titles and she was a picture of strength, so good at using her body. When I was playing the game, I don't think many knew how to use their body like the Germans. They were physically strong and they had a style and system that was so difficult to play against.

I wasn't the only player to have a break out tournament in 2007, there was also a Brazilian who some may know quite well, Marta.

She was a game-winner. She could make defenders look silly with her technical ability and her speed, and the way she used her hips to move past players. She is, as of this writing, the six-time World Player of the Year and a player unlike any the sport has ever seen – or may ever see again.

She has been the number one talent for a number of years. She has that Brazilian flair where she is so good technically, the ball is stuck to her like glue. She can create those moments that get you out of your seat.

I was often compared to Marta, especially back in 2007 when we both had a stand out tournament. To be compared to and play against her, even though we never really came up against each other because we're both so high up on the pitch, was a real compliment. She has been the best player for a long time, and after Mia Hamm and Prinz, she is the player everyone knows about.

In 2011, Marta's Brazil opened against Australia, who had won only one match at the World Cup before, against Ghana in 2007. They really kicked on after that and in Germany four years later, they had what I guess you could describe as a golden generation of players coming through. Sam Kerr, Caitlin Foord, Emily Van Egmond: teenagers who were given a chance by their coach Tom Sermanni, who clearly saw something special in them. That's almost unheard of in this day and age. I made my debut for England at seventeen, but that's because there was no youth structure in the build-up to the senior side. So to be given that opportunity, and for them to have grasped it and taken it on, does not come easy.

For them, and for every other player featured in this book, they've lived their dream. Not everyone has the opportunity to represent their country, sing the national anthem with pride, and go and create memories.

Playing in a World Cup was the highlight of my career. Yes there was heartache, but to say you have played in two World Cups, and to say you have represented your country and have been on that journey, is a dream come true.

I hope you enjoy the stories that Kieran and Jeff have been able to tell. I'm sure they will bring back some fond memories and provide perspective you may not have previously had.

Kelly Smith, MBE

The Early Years

....

It was 1986 when Norwegian delegate Ellen Wille took the microphone at the 45th FIFA Congress in Mexico City. Wille – whose country was among the few with relatively established women's soccer teams – was demanding change. The first men's World Cup was held in 1930 and now, over fifty years later, the women still didn't have a sanctioned event. FIFA (*Fédération Internationale de Football Association*), world soccer's governing body, wasn't doing enough for the women's game. Now, Wille needed to convince a group of a hundred-plus men of that.

'I'd had to fight to get women's football recognised in Norway, and I wanted to continue that internationally,' Wille would tell FIFA Media decades later. 'So, I took to the stage at the FIFA Congress, and pointed out that women's football was mentioned nowhere in any of the documents. I also said it was high time the women had their own World Cup and took part in the Olympic Football Tournament.'

FIFA president João Havelange agreed, and the wheels were put into motion to change this. A test event dubbed the FIFA Women's Invitational Tournament was held in China in 1988. Twelve teams from six continents were invited to take part in the tournament which Norway won, defeating Sweden, 1-0 in the final behind a goal from Linda Medalen. The most important result, however, was the overall success of the tournament.[*]

* https://www.fifa.com/womensworldcup/news/ellen-wille-mother-norwegian-women-football-1462830 & https://www.youtube.com/watch?v=OkJ4nXznUVg

Play on the field was up to par and the support in the stands strong enough that FIFA decided to hold its first official women's version of the World Cup in 1991, which China would again host. Even that first official tournament was something of a trial run, however.

Confectionary company Mars Inc. was the official sponsor of the event, so while 1991 is now commonly referenced as the World Cup, at the time it was officially dubbed the 'First FIFA World Championship for Women's Football for the M&Ms Cup'. Talk about a mouthful. The lack of the much more straightforward term, 'World Cup', was seen by players as a slight, an indication that FIFA wasn't so sure about holding the event – and didn't want it to take away from the prestige of the men's World Cup.

'We had to first convince them that they should do this,' said midfielder Julie Foudy, who played for the United States at that first World Cup and in the three which followed. 'They didn't want to call it the World Cup, because they felt it would infringe on the men. Literally,' she laughs, 'they sold it.'

Alternative rules reinforced players' suspicions of sexism. The event would be condensed into just two weeks; the 1990 men's World Cup, with twice the number of teams, took place over thirty-one days. Matches would last only eighty minutes rather than the standard ninety minutes. FIFA appeared to be worried that women players couldn't handle the extra ten minutes. Or, as US captain April Heinrichs would tell *Sports Illustrated* years later: 'They were afraid our ovaries were going to fall out if we played ninety.'[*]

So, a women's version of the World Cup had arrived. Expectations, however, were non-existent. It was nearly impossible to scout opponents – games were often unofficial, and the internet as we know it didn't yet exist. European teams knew a little more

* https://www.si.com/longform/soccer-goals/goal4.html

about each other due to proximity, but countries like the United States, Brazil, Nigeria and New Zealand were the lone representatives from their respective continents. They were left largely to develop their own styles.

There were, however, unofficial world events which predated FIFA's awakening to the women's game. Italy hosted the 'Coppa del Mondo' in 1970 – considered by some as the first unofficial women's world championship – which was a European tournament plus Mexico. Denmark would defeat the hosts in the final in front of an estimated forty thousand fans in Torino.*

One year later, Mexico hosted another unsanctioned women's world championship. Six teams split into two groups – Argentina, Denmark, England, France, Italy and Mexico – converged upon Mexico City and Guadalajara one year after Mexico hosted the men's World Cup. Cheap tickets and a rich soccer culture in Mexico generated unprecedented interest. An estimated 110,000 fans were in attendance at Estadio Azteca to see Denmark defeat the hosts in the final. Sponsorship – not FIFA – could largely be thanked for footing the bill and making the event possible.†

From there, the 'Mundialito' ('Little World Cup') invitational tournament was held in Italy each year from 1984 to 1988. It was at that tournament, on 18 August 1985, that the United States women's national team played its first official match – a 1-0 loss to Italy in Jesolo. The Americans would tie Denmark, lose to England and lose to Denmark in a rematch before heading home. This was the most exposure the Americans would get to outside competition before returning home and training individually. They wouldn't even play another official match for nearly a full year. Thoughts of any sort of formal World Cup were nonexistent.

* http://www.rsssf.com/tablesm/mondo-women70.html
† https://www.bbc.com/news/business-46149887

'You just played for your national team,' Heinrichs said. 'I don't know that we thought of a World Cup or a destination yet, because there were barely even friendlies. There was one tournament that we were aware of, and that was the Mundialito in Italy. We played in that for two years and then just started waiting for the next invitation and the next opportunity at a tournament. Who we were going to play didn't matter.'

A lack of expectations combined with relative youth made for a very informal start for the United States women's programme. Mia Hamm, Kristine Lilly and Julie Foudy – players who would go on to create enduring legacies in 1999 and who would play into the new millennium – were only teenagers when they joined the team in the late 1980s. From the teens right up to more veteran players like Carin Jennings and Michelle Akers, the idea that they were doing anything more than playing one-off soccer games was lost on them.

'It was just fun for us,' said Jennings – now Carin Gabarra. 'I'm a total product of Title XI. I grew up having no female sports – none of that, no opportunity. And all of a sudden, this stuff started coming around, right at the end of my college days. Everyone just loved it because we just loved playing. We weren't over-playing then. There weren't even major amounts of high school teams or college programmes or any of that yet. It was all new for us.'

Anson Dorrance, however, was aware of the unique situation the Americans found themselves in as unknown challengers from outside the European elite.

'What we had an opportunity to do, which was unique, was we got to develop our game within the sort of cultural and athletic mores of the United States,' says Dorrance, who guided the US to the 1991 World Cup crown. 'And if you look at those qualities, the Americans do have a unique kind of style or bias – whatever you want to call it. So, for me, I was coaching entirely within the parameters of our own culture. Because we had no culture, we couldn't pride ourselves on our sophistication or our creativity. But we had this relentless, irrepressible American spirit with a confidence that belied our capability. We had this extraordinary optimism. If you look at our history, it's a history of this extraordinary confidence without any reason for why you would have it. We sort of built upon that, and we built upon things that we could control.'

From there, the culture of the United States women's national team was born.

Many confuse Dorrance with being the first coach in the history of the US women's programme. That honour goes to Mike Ryan, who coached the team for its winless four-game trip to Italy in 1985. Dorrance, who was at the time already the coach of the University of North Carolina men's and women's programmes, was brought on as coach of the US women – a part-time role.

His task was not enviable: build a team with limited budgets, no regular training camps and few international matches. Individual practice would make up the bulk of training time for players, which meant that their strengths were going to be one-v-one and fitness.

'We developed a culture of young women that were wonderfully self-disciplined,' Dorrance says. 'They had to get fit on their own, they had to develop their own training environments – just because we didn't have camps; we couldn't invest in them – and we had to develop a team without playing a lot. So, it wasn't like we came into that '91 and all these players had numerous caps like the Norwegians and the Swedes. But we came in with something else: we came in with just an overriding confidence that we were going to win a particular way.'

Born was a culture which endures today: an American game which, while it has evolved and become more tactically and technically disciplined, is rooted in hard work and athleticism.

That Dorrance was also in charge of North Carolina's women's team would prove beneficial. North Carolina set the standard in women's soccer, winning the first three National Collegiate Athletic Association women's soccer championships from 1982 to 1984 and then winning an astounding nine consecutive national titles from 1986 to 1994.

Nine of the players who filled out the eighteen-player roster for the United States at that inaugural World Cup had played for Dorrance in some capacity at North Carolina. In lieu of formal training camps under US Soccer, Dorrance was able to instil an aggressive, attacking style of play in his North Carolina teams that he would test and refine before bringing to the international stage. He'd see something the US needed to work on while on international duty, make note of it, search for answers when he had more training time with North Carolina, and then bring solutions back to the international stage. It was a cycle.

'When I would finish an event with the US women, I would come back to UNC and say, "Alright, we had trouble with this, we had trouble with that,"' he said. 'And this would be an incubation training camp for how we were going to try to solve problems in the international arena.'

What he was developing was a style of play that women's soccer wasn't accustomed to – one which would serve as the framework for future generations of American players.

European teams played with similar, pragmatic styles: four defenders, four midfielders and two forwards. It was a slow, methodical game based on possession. Teams would swing the ball around the back, look for an opening, and if none presented itself, they would reset and try again. Few questioned at the time that this was the way to play soccer. Norway and Sweden were considered the world's elite, and this is how they played.

None of that suited the Americans, however. They didn't have a rich soccer culture guiding them on a certain way to play the game. They had few outside influences and little time to train foreign concepts, so they took a more radical approach. They were going to play three defenders in the back – two marking and one sweeping – with four midfielders and three forwards. *Three forwards?* What would become a norm in the modern game felt like a preposterous idea at the time, except the Americans had little criticism to face. They didn't garner any media attention and there existed no expectations. The team was still relatively new and the sport generally off the radar of mainstream press.

So, the US began developing its game, emphasising holistic defensive pressure from everyone on the team – starting with the three forwards – and the unique individual skills of their attacking players. The Americans' plan, developed almost in secret in the late 1980s and deployed for the world to see in 1991, was to reach out and choke the other teams with relentless energy.

'We had three players up there who were freaking carnivores, and if you're passing the ball around them, you're going to get a piece of your thigh ripped off,' Dorrance said.

So they pressed. And when they'd win the ball, they would 'start carving', as Dorrance put it. Akers, Heinrichs and Jennings on the front line; Hamm, Lilly and Foudy joined by Shannon Higgins in the middle. The United States' front seven players at that 1991 World Cup were a collection of one-v-one geniuses who were ready and willing to face any defender. The team's style of play suited them and they suited the system.

Internally, the group was confident. Externally, they were nobodies. They earned $10 per diem and most players couldn't hold regular jobs, because they were away too often and too sporadically with the national team. Foudy recalls telling her parents about the forthcoming inaugural World Cup, and they didn't know what she was talking about. She returned home that December to Stanford University professors wondering where she had been.

Outside US borders, the traditional soccer countries with deep-rooted histories in the men's game didn't take the Americans seriously. And why should they? The US had no significant history in the sport. The US men's team's qualification for the 1990 World Cup ended a forty-year absence from the tournament.

All the circumstances added up to give the US the type of surprise factor that they were hoping would jar teams. The question remained: would it work?

The date 16 November 1991 marked the first match in official, FIFA-sanctioned history of the Women's World Cup. Hosts China defeated Norway 4-0 in front of a crowd of sixty-five thousand fans. The Americans arrived that November familiar with their surroundings – perhaps too familiar. They had been there in 1987 and then again for the test invitational event in 1988, when they lost to eventual champions Norway in the quarter-finals. And they played three games in six days there against the hosts in August 1991 to further assimilate. Those trips were invaluable in teaching the players how to deal with the culture shock of life *off* the field while on the road.

American players found it tough to adapt to the Chinese diet, particularly on a budget. Players resorted to Snickers-and-Pepsi diets during the 1988 test event – hardly the breakfast of champions. But US players found that they couldn't stomach the local food. This predated the modern, hyper-controlled team environments in which professional clubs and international teams build entire support teams around nutrition and sports science. In the late 1980s and early '90s, you ate what you found.

'In the World Cup, there were pretty much staples of food that you didn't explore,' Heinrichs said. 'I looked up and there were worms all over my broccoli. I had already eaten most of the plate, so I was freaking out. I didn't eat broccoli for like five years.'

Having learned their lessons, the Americans brought their own chefs over to the 1991 Women's World Cup. On a budget, that meant volunteer family members: Dorrance's brother and defender Carla Werden's soon-to-be husband. The pair brought with them packets of pasta which the team ate religiously, topped with whatever sauce they could find. Such a basic meal became a delicacy to the Americans – and they weren't alone.

Sweden would serve as the Americans' first-ever World Cup opponent on 17 November 1991. The teams appeared to have little in common. Staying in the same hotel in Panyu, however, revealed one common bond: the food. The Swedes seemingly weren't as prepared as the Americans for the culture shock. When they found out that the US camp had the delicacy that was plain pasta, they inquired about obtaining some . . . right before the teams were to play one another.

'So here it is, they are our rivals in this World Cup – and one of the best teams in the world, by the way – and we open [the tournament] with them,' Dorrance recalls. 'We only beat them 3-2. So it wasn't like, "Should we share this with them? They might beat us." We knew they could beat us! But back then, again, we were part of a culture trying to promote the game internationally, so we fed them.'

Multiple trips to China in the years leading up to the 1991 tournament hardened many of the Americans towards the country. Bottled water served many purposes: drunk straight, it was standard hydration. Adding a pack of Kool-Aide mix was a treat for players. They used bottled water to brush their teeth.

There was also the matter of travelling on a budget. Heinrichs recalls how the team arrived in China for the August tournament before the World Cup. The team got in late – near midnight, as she recalls – and were already staying three players to a room when one side of their hotel began flooding. So players migrated into the rooms of teammates across the hall – putting up to six to a room – and slept on their duffel bags, which they hadn't yet unpacked.

And then there was the time Heinrichs went to use the bathroom on a train in China: it was just a hole in the floor of the train. 'You could look down and see the tracks.' China wasn't the only place from which the Americans had stories, it was just a frequent stop in their early travels. There was also the Bulgaria-based airplane that had a smoking and non-smoking section – with no divider.

Heinrichs likened herself to the popular 1970s children's toys, the egg-shaped dolls called Weebles. 'Weebles wobble, but they don't fall down,' the toy's catchy jingle went. She developed it as a personal mantra.

'It was a real "deal with it" mentality,' she said. 'It didn't faze our players – that's when I say old school. We didn't complain about it. We were not the generation that was fighting for equal pay or equal opportunity. We were nowhere close. We were the generation that was – deal with it, adapt, keep moving forward, fight for and earn everything you are going to get. Consequently, we didn't get bothered by a hotel that didn't have good food or that wasn't right.'

Such struggles weren't unique to the United States. Women's soccer was still a fledgling sport globally. Funding and support were nowhere near that of the men's game – or even anything close to offering a living wage.

What the Americans did feel was that they had prepared

themselves for the harsh realities better than some of the other national teams. Their formation as a programme just five years earlier came over a decade after some of the best European teams played their first official international matches. The Americans – a mix of green teenagers and relatively inexperienced 'veterans' – to that point had next to nothing for support, so, as a result, they expected nothing. That allowed them to adapt to humbling conditions easily – and Jennings believes that it was a key ingredient to their World Cup triumph.

'We got $10 per day. Food, it was what we were given on the road – whatever was culturally acceptable to give us,' she said. 'That was part of the mystique and part of our growth. If we weren't prepared for some of the cultural differences, I don't know that we could have walked into a World Cup in 1991 and spent three whole weeks in China and done so well, because it's difficult. It's quite different and there were a lot of changes and a lot of things accepted. In that case, we were a lot more acclimatised than anyone else.'

That appeared to be the case early. The US opened up a 3-0 lead on Sweden in the opening match before conceding twice late to make things interesting. A 5-0 victory over Brazil followed, and the Americans rounded out group play with a 3-0 victory over Japan. Then came a 7-0 victory over Chinese Taipei in the quarter-finals which saw Michelle Akers score five goals: still a tournament record for a single match.

Now, the Americans had the world's attention. And they had their platform: powerhouse Germany awaited in the semi-finals.

Akers' five-goal performance in the quarter-final provided a window into the dominance of the Americans' progressive style of play. The three-forward front line that Dorrance had implemented was doing exactly what he had hoped. Akers had eight goals through the first four matches of the tournament, with Jennings adding three and Heinrichs scoring twice.

Teams were rattled by the Americans' high-pressure approach. These were the final days when goalkeepers could still pick the ball up with their hands if their own defender passed it back to them, a rule which was changed in 1992 in reaction to the negative tactics used at the 1990 men's World Cup. The old rule encouraged teams to keep the ball in the back and build methodically. If they ever got into trouble, they could pass it back to their goalkeeper to grab the ball and start afresh.*

Akers, Heinrichs and Jennings, in particular, challenged that comfort and created goals directly off interceptions in opposing teams' defensive areas of the field. The unique culture that the Americans had cultivated on their own metaphoric island, away from the influences of European teams, was working. And it wasn't just working; it was entertaining.

'We served FIFA in a way,' Dorrance said. 'Because then all of a sudden, it wasn't like a public relations project to sell the fact that this was a great World Cup – it was reality. They saw that we were a very attractive product. Goal-scoring, attacking, just smothering opponents. We served FIFA, we served the international game. Because then these countries went back with our style, and we were the beginning of gaining a respect for the women's game in the world.'

Crowds were relatively impressive – ten thousand-plus for group-stage matches and sixty-three thousand for the final – though it was widely assumed that factory workers in their thousands were ordered to attend matches and root for teams, including the US – American flags in hand and all. China, it would soon be revealed,

---

* https://www.theguardian.com/football/2015/feb/18/knowledge-last-goalkeeper-legally-pick-up-backpass

was angling to bring the 2000 Summer Olympic Games to Beijing – a vote it would narrowly lose to Sydney, Australia, in 1993 – and the government was motivated to put on a grand event at the 1991 Women's World Cup.

Despite that, there was still genuine attention on the Americans thanks to their style of play. Chinese media took notice of how effective the US front three was, dubbing the combination of Akers, Heinrichs and Jennings 'The Triple-Edged Sword' for how they carved apart defences.

Akers was a powerful forward – a pure finisher in the air. Heinrichs was fit and widely lauded by teammates as ultra-competitive: losing wasn't an option. Jennings – nicknamed 'Crazy Legs' – was the dribbler. She could score or create. Each player complemented the other, creating a dynamic attack with no obvious area of focus for opposing defences.

'The three of us, we had a really mutual respect about the way we knew we complemented each other and the way that it would be difficult for a team to manage us,' Heinrichs said. 'We have a little bit of a benefit of looking back now, but we had no idea going into the World Cup if we were going to be successful.'

A pre-tournament injury to Megan McCarthy shuffled the United States' lineup in China, but that front seven – along with Joy Biefeld (Fawcett), Carla Werden (Overbeck) and Linda Hamilton in defence, plus Mary Harvey in goal – really hit their stride in the knockout stage. Germany was a new kind of test, however.

Gero Bisanz was the head coach of Germany's women's national team and was also the director of the German Football Association's coaches training facilities. He was the coach who trained coaches in Germany; he wrote the book on coaching in that country for four decades. And here, on the first official world stage for the women, he was out to show that the Germans' style of keeping possession was definitively the best approach to the sport.

'I read his books,' Dorrance says proudly. 'I knew exactly what he was going to do. We reached out and crushed them.'

Jennings scored a hat-trick in the opening thirty-three minutes of that semi-final as the Americans throttled an overwhelmed Germany. Her first goal came ten minutes into the match when she pounced on a poor German back pass and showed composure one-v-one with German goalkeeper Marion Isbert, tucking the ball into the net with the outside of her foot.

Jennings' second goal was a stunner. Mia Hamm collected the ball on the sideline after a German turnover near midfield. Hamm played a quick ball to Jennings, who took three touches and fired a right-footed shot from 25 yards into the far upper corner, freezing Isbert, who could only watch it go into the net.

Completing the hat-trick was once again a matter of the United States' high pressure exposing the methodical Germans. Akers applied pressure on the right side and forced Germany to play the ball centrally. Under pressure, the pass was again off the mark; Jennings collected the ball, dribbled toward goal and calmly tucked it into the lower corner. The Germans were shell-shocked. Heidi Mohr would get a goal back for Germany one minute later, but Heinrichs scored twice in the second half as the US stormed into the first Women's World Cup final with a 5-2 victory over Germany.

Proof of concept. The Americans now had it. 'That was the game where the culmination of our ideas blossomed,' Dorrance says. Bisanz was humiliated. Hammered by the unknown Americans, Bisanz, as Dorrance remembers, was incredulous after the loss. Dorrance was flattered by how much his team rattled the incumbent powers.

Jennings' performance went a long way in earning her the Golden Ball as the tournament's best player. 'First of all, none of us even knew there were awards,' she said. 'It wasn't something we played for or asked for.' She said she'll always remember that hat-trick. She had just become engaged to Jim Gabarra, captain of the US national futsal team and pro indoor soccer star, and he had made the trip to China to see the team play the semi-final in person. Jennings had to get special permission from Dorrance to break the team rule: no family visits on game day. The Triple-Edged Sword carved up its most prominent victim yet. Now, Norway stood between the United States and the first Women's World Cup trophy.

Akers' time to shine was the final. Her header in the twentieth minute was an emphatic display of power and put the Americans ahead early. Nine minutes later, however, Norway answered on a free kick and header of their own. Norwegian star Linda Medalen rose above a pack of players to head the ball off the post and into the net for the equaliser.

Akers knew that she needed to take the game by its throat. Goalkeeper coach Tony DiCicco, who would succeed Dorrance as head coach, had a message for Akers coming out of half-time: 'You're going to have to win the game.' He was serious, and she knew it.[*]

Flash-forward to the seventy-eighth minute, just two minutes until the full-time whistle in this abbreviated, eighty-minute match setup that FIFA implemented for the first Women's World Cup. Midfielder Shannon Higgins receives the ball inside her own half of the centre circle and facing her own goal. In one smooth motion, she settles the ball with her right foot and turns toward Norway's goal, looking up to see her options. She launches a hopeful ball forward toward Akers which is intercepted by Norwegian defender Tina Svensson, who is now facing her own goal. Feeling pressure on her back from Akers, Svensson plays the ball back to her goalkeeper – and Akers pounces.

[*] https://www.si.com/longform/soccer-goals/goal4.html

Realising the pass back lacks enough weight to reach its intended target, Akers jumps in, beating Norwegian goalkeeper Reidun Seth to the ball. Akers takes a touch around Seth and has an open net, but her momentum is taking her away from goal. She takes an extra touch with her left foot to compose herself and passes the ball into the net with her right foot. The goal is Akers' tournament-leading tenth, and it's the final tally at this inaugural Women's World Cup. Fittingly, it was another product of the team's high-pressure approach that clinched the title for the Americans.

US players and staff celebrated on the field and returned to their hotel, where the four semi-finalists were staying. Sweden had defeated Germany 4-0 in the third-place match the day prior, and the Swedes were only in that game after a 4-1 defeat to bitter rival Norway in the semi-final. The Swedes also hadn't forgotten about their pre-tournament pasta dinner.

'When I got off the elevator after we were world champions,' Dorrance recalls, 'and the doors to the elevator opened, the Swedish gold socks were spread to say "congratulations" right in front of the elevator.'

Dorrance's coaching staff always made it a point to tell their players that they were 'soccer evangelists' who needed to sell the sport. A small gesture of pasta, and a small congratulations in return, was a glimpse into what he meant. The first FIFA Women's World Cup was a success.

Returning home to the US was humbling for the Americans. They flew the long way home, connecting in Europe to land in New York before going their separate ways. They were met at the airport by only a handful of people – one of them the US men's national team coach at the time, Bora Milutinovic. Most of the country didn't know that the event had even taken place. Even those who cared had to get news of results with a significant delay, with no internet or live television options.

Juxtapose that humble scene with the huge, New York City tickertape parade that celebrated the United States' third World Cup triumph, in 2015, and the dissonance is striking. That first generation of American players was unfazed, however. Nobody had ever had a welcome-home victory parade, so nobody expected a parade. There was nothing to miss.

'We didn't play for the recognition,' Heinrichs said. 'We didn't play for the money. We played for the opportunity to put ourselves against the best in the world and hopefully to one day call ourselves the best in the world. That's what motivated me. Waking up thinking, "OK, if there's someone out there working harder than me, I better work harder. If there's a team out there better than us, we need to work harder. If all of us improve by 1 per cent, we'll get better."

'So, just this thought that you are comparing yourself against somebody out there in the world that is working as hard as you are, so what are you going to do to get the edge was kind of what motivated us and our generation of players. I call them the '91ers. The '91ers are different than the '99ers. It was an older generation, an older-school approach. Very similar styles.'

The '91ers set the table for everything that was to follow. The United States has ever since been a dominant force in women's soccer, in 2015 becoming the first programme to win three Women's World Cup titles in just the seventh edition of the tournament. The Americans won four of the first five Olympic gold medals in the sport, including the inaugural women's soccer competition on home soil in 1996.

Without the success of China – the entire tournament, not just the Americans' part – perhaps none of that would have happened. 'FIFA wanted to hide this World Cup in case it failed,' Dorrance recalls of 1991. The establishment of a World Cup paved the way for women's soccer to become an Olympic sport beginning at the 1996 Atlanta Summer Games.

China 1991 sparked the rivalries which would dominate the first decade of FIFA-sanctioned women's international competitions. The Americans would meet Norway again at the 1995 World Cup in Sweden, this time in the semi-finals. Ann Aarones' goal in the tenth minute sunk the United States' hopes of repeating, and Norway's famous 'train' celebration after the match made the Americans' blood boil; they felt disrespected.

US players carried that image with them into the 1996 Olympics, and when they met Norway again in the semi-finals of that competition, they rallied from a goal down early to win in extra-time. Shannon MacMillan scored the Golden Goal that day in front of a crowd of nearly sixty-five thousand in Athens, Georgia. Over seventy-six thousand fans watched the US defeat China for the gold medal four days later. The commercial success of that tournament, in part, inspired confidence that the 1999 World Cup to be held in the US could indeed support a more ambitious plan to play in larger venues. That 1999 tournament became the gold standard in women's sporting events.

There was a clear domino effect in the decade which followed. That can be traced back to the success of the 1991 tournament as a whole – the attacking soccer which produced ninety-nine goals in twenty-six matches, and China's efforts to fill the stands.

And from the perspective of the United States, a sporting juggernaut was born.

'I think it was the start of the US women's national team programme and the start of a programme that won three World Cups and four Olympic gold medals,' Jennings says of 1991. 'That was the start of the culture of the US women's national team. That culture has never wavered. That is a culture of mentality, competitiveness and hard work, along with talent. So, I think it was the start of that. That has always been there. Every person who has ever played for the US national team is connected in that regard.'

The Birth of the Lionesses

It was 18 July 2013 in Linkoping, Sweden, when a relentless and classy France team swept aside an uninspiring England in a 3-0 victory that saw Hope Powell's side finish bottom of their European Championship group, and subsequently crash out of the tournament with just one point from their three matches.

This, coming four years after Powell had led her side to the EURO 2009 final in Finland, where they finished runners-up, and two years after the 2011 World Cup in Germany, where her side had reached the quarter-finals, losing to France on penalties.

The EUROs in Sweden were seen as another stepping stone to England joining the elite sides that had frustrated them on so many occasions over the years – but they had failed.

A lacklustre, lethargic England side would be heading home before the knockout stages, and all of a sudden, after fifteen years in charge, Powell's position was now under scrutiny having been so influential in propelling England to its current status.

It was one month later, on 20 August 2013, that Powell was sacked by the English Football Association, and her fifteen-year reign as head coach of the national team had come to an end.

In a statement released by the League Managers' Association, Powell said on her dismissal: 'I leave very honoured to have contributed to all of the collective achievements of the group over the past 15 years.

'The women's game as a whole has made significant progress during this time and will continue to do so in years to come. I am extremely proud to have played some part in the development of women's football as a whole.'*

It was the end of an era. For many of England's players, playing under Powell was all they knew at international level. She had overseen significant change from top to bottom in England's football pyramid, with few summarising her impact better than the *Guardian*'s Anna Kessel, who wrote after Powell's dismissal: 'Powell's achievements in modernising women's football in this country are heroic, awe-inspiring and downright revolutionary. Powell in the boardroom, say insiders, was a force to be reckoned with. For any woman – let alone a black woman – to take on the pale, male and stale suits of the governing body who had little interest in or regard for women's football, and demand investment, demand a youth structure, demand central contracts, demand an elite environment in which female footballers could develop, demand parity in medical expertise, should not be underestimated. Powell had to fight prehistoric attitudes and she came up trumps.'†

But it was time for a new era, a new beginning, and a new birth of the England team. Powell's departure came almost a year after the FA had opened its brand-new training headquarters in the centre of the country, St George's Park.

As outlined on the FA's website, 'This £105m facility, set in 330-acres of Staffordshire countryside, is the home to England's twenty-eight national teams. With thirteen outdoor pitches, including a replica of the Wembley surface, a full-size indoor 3G pitch, a suite of rehabilitation and sports science areas, and an indoor futsal sports hall, St George's Park provides world-class facilities for all England teams ahead of international fixtures.'

---

* https://www.bbc.co.uk/sport/football/23768854
† https://www.theguardian.com/football/blog/2013/aug/22/hope-powell-england-players

The key term in all of that is 'all England teams', meaning England's women's team, for the first time, would have access to world-class facilities that would allow them to try and close the gap on the teams above them.

One person who would be involved in overseeing the transition to St George's Park was Kay Cossington, Head of Women's National Development Teams. Cossington, who has been with the FA since 2007, worked with Hope Powell to get the right pieces in place to ensure the facilities available to the players were complemented by the right staff.

'We now have a world-class, world-leading facility, but the structure and people within that facility are what has made it special,' said Cossington.

'Pre St George's Park we had an internal identity that factored in playing styles, philosophies and player behaviour, but that was driven more by what Hope wanted, rather than what we believed was right coming from a high-performance environment.

'Now it's about high performance. How we plan, how we deliver, how we educate and how we work as a team. St George's Park has given us the opportunity to start to live in a high-performing culture and environment, and we have been trying to see how that plays out under a number of different disciplines.'

With Hope Powell gone, attention turned to the 2015 World Cup, which was being held in Canada. Brent Hills, who had worked as Powell's assistant, would oversee the opening few fixtures of qualification. There was certainly a feeling amongst some that Hills should get the role full-time, being that he knew the players and the setup. But for others, the view was it was time for a new era, a new dawn, and a new vision.

The FA invited applicants for the role, with some of the game's biggest names linked with replacing Powell. Canada's John Herdman, US-based coach Paul Riley, from Liverpool, and former

World Cup winning coach, Tony DiCicco*, who sadly passed away in 2017, were all reported to be interested in taking on the job.

Another who submitted an application, was Bristol Academy Head Coach, Mark Sampson. The Welsh Coach had just seen his team finish runners-up in the FA Women's Super League, which meant for the first time, they would be playing in the UEFA Women's Champions League.

At just thirty-one-years-old, Sampson was by far the most inexperienced of the candidates, but after impressing the interview panel, which included former England international Trevor Brooking, Sampson was announced as England's second full-time head coach on 6 December 2013.

'Women's football in England is in a fantastic place right now, with the growth and development of the game in the last few years, and I am ready to give everything I have to build a team that every English supporter can be proud of,' Sampson said on his appointment.

The challenge now for Sampson was to instil his philosophy and playing style on a team who had only worked under two coaches, Hope Powell and Brent Hills, over the previous fifteen years, and one of those had only been in interim charge for a few months.

Sampson would be able to call on the support of Hills, if needed, when Powell's former assistant was appointed to fill a newly created role that was formed as part of the FA's 'Game Changer' strategy, launched in 2012.

Hills would fill the position of Head of Women's Elite Development, which formed part of the newly launched Elite Performance Unit. The strategy outlined that Hills would be overseeing a unit that 'will drive the strategic development of the player

---

* DiCicco confirmed in an interview with the author of this chapter in 2014 that he did speak to the FA about the role.

and coach pathways to help build winning teams. It will be able to take advantage of the facilities, infrastructure, personnel and services at St George's Park. The EPU will now hold the remit to develop the best young players. A Head of Elite Women's Development will be responsible for the talent pathway, including producing more and better coaches working in the women's game at all levels.'

With a World Cup on the horizon, this was a positive move by the FA as they looked to close the gap on the sides above them, with Sampson taking on a team that sat outside the world's top ten and was still licking its wounds after early EURO 2013 elimination.

His first big decision would be to select his captain, with the unenviable task of potentially removing the armband from Casey Stoney, who had led England at the EUROs and Team GB at the London Olympics in 2012.

Stoney had been a stalwart of the England team, having made over a hundred appearances and played in four major tournaments for her country. More importantly, she had the respect of her team-mates and was largely expected to retain the armband.

Sampson had other ideas, and made a significant statement in handing the captaincy to Manchester City defender, Steph Houghton, in April 2014.

Houghton had been a regular in Hope Powell's squads but was rarely given the opportunity to shine in her preferred positions of centre-back or holding midfield.

It was a leap of faith by Sampson, who had given Houghton the captaincy in two friendlies against Norway at the start of 2014, and then against Canada at the Cyprus Cup two months later.

It's a conversation that Houghton remembers well, going into it with absolutely no expectation that she would be leading her country into World Cup qualifiers, and potentially a World Cup the following year.

'I'd just moved to City and I had been given the armband, but in terms of my international career I was nowhere near being a regular starter. So for me I just wanted to make sure I was in the squad. Mark said he saw me as a leader of his team, but obviously there were a lot of candidates like Fara Williams and Jill Scott, who had played a number of times for England, Kelly Smith was still involved at that time, and of course Casey, who was current captain. The conversation was about how the next three or four months would go. We had the Cyprus Cup coming up and that would be an opportunity to impress. I will always remember sitting down with him at St George's Park around April. I'd had the armband a few times and no way did I think it would be a possibility for the long term, but I remember him saying what I brought to the team and the sort of things he was looking for in his captain, and then he asked me if I would take the role and be the leader of the team. Obviously, you're delighted but the rest of the conversation was a bit of a blur.'

It was a sign of how far Houghton had come, not just by being made captain, but also by working her way into a position that would see her become an established member of the team having missed both the 2007 World Cup and 2009 EUROs due to career threatening injuries.

If selected, Houghton would have been the youngest England player at the 2007 World Cup but, two days before the squad flew to China, she broke a leg in training. Two years later, shortly before the squad was announced for the European Championships, she ruptured cruciate ligaments while at Leeds United.

Houghton was twenty-five when Sampson named her captain, and that comes with pressure. As she mentioned, there were experienced heads, in some cases much more experienced, and she would have to lead players who were used to leading.

Houghton admitted that, at first, she found this a challenge, and confessed that she understood that some may have seen the decision by Sampson as the wrong one.

'It's difficult. I think if you asked if I played my best football in them first six months of being captain, I think I'd probably say no. I put a little bit too much pressure on myself, I tried to please everyone in the squad, staff included, and that was impossible to do.

'Looking back now it drains a lot of energy and ultimately, your focus is taken away from being a footballer. I think first and foremost, because I was so young and there were experienced players in the squad, I think there may have been a feeling amongst some that it was the wrong decision, and I totally get that. I have been part of teams where you're thinking, "that's a bit of a strange decision," but I totally respect people for having their opinions.

'I think as time went on, I worked really hard on my development. I took the hours away from the pitch to develop what kind of leader I wanted to be. Ultimately that was to lead by example and be the person that I am on and off the pitch, and to be approachable. I have the utmost respect for those senior players because they have paved the way for the youngsters coming through. For me it wasn't working against them, it was a case of using their experience and using them as fellow leaders to create a team environment and a special environment where we loved playing for England.'

The captaincy was one change that Sampson made, but he also freshened the squad up during World Cup qualification, giving younger players such as Arsenal's Jordan Nobbs and Liverpool's Lucy Bronze more of a starting role, and bringing back forwards Natasha Dowie and Lianne Sanderson, who had both been left out during Hope Powell's later years in charge of England.

That expansion of the player pool meant that England's players now needed to stay on their toes, as regularly under Powell you could predict her squad of twenty-three and get the majority correct. Certainly in the early days under Sampson, it wasn't that simple.

However, Houghton was quick to point out that increased player depth mirrored changes in the game, with Sampson having a much wider group to select from, which is even more applicable now.

'I think with Hope, in terms of the strength in depth we had compared to what she had to work with, the coaching we get, we're full-time professionals now. If you use Kelly Smith as an example, we don't just have that standout player. There is a smaller gap in terms of quality, which is credit to the coaches in this country and to the girls as well.

'Hope had her strongest XI and a team that she trusted, but there was always one or two that could try and fight their way into that starting XI. But I think with Mark, he was quite flexible with the system – he played the cards that suited the game plan that he wanted to play. That was credit to him that he trusted the girls, but also the girls being able to adapt to the system that he wanted us to play.'

Sampson's approach when he took the job was to open the door and allow players to feel they had a chance of going to a World Cup. That was looking all the more possible with results on the field. England had already won four of their qualifiers before Sampson's arrival against Belarus (6-0), Turkey (8-0 & 4-0) and Wales (2-0), when he took charge of his first competitive game at home to Montenegro at Brighton's AMEX Stadium.

A 9-0 victory over the minnows showed a no mercy approach by the new England boss as his side overran their part-time opponents, but if fans and the media were hoping to gain an idea of what Sampson was going to bring to the role, this was not the match to judge him on.

In fact, it was hard to judge him or his team or their credentials from their entire qualifying campaign, as they coasted against largely inferior opposition, with Wales and Ukraine being their only real tests. They finished with a qualifying record of played ten, won ten, scored fifty-two, conceded . . . one! Striker Eni Aluko managed to score more goals (thirteen) in qualifying, than Turkey, Belarus and Montenegro were able to muster in total through their entire campaigns.

The argument will be that you can only beat the opposition in front of you, and Sampson's team had done that convincingly, booking their place at England's fourth World Cup since the country's debut at the 1995 tournament.

The draw for the 2015 Women's World Cup would take place on 6 December 2014 in Ottawa at the Canadian Museum of History. England, due to their world ranking, would not be one of the seeded teams, which would mean they would have to face one of: hosts Canada, world champions Japan, Germany, the United States, France or Brazil. Whoever they faced, it would be a daunting task.

Sampson's side would be drawn with and open the tournament against France, who they had not beaten in forty-one years, along with Colombia and Mexico, the latter a side they had drawn with at the 2011 World Cup 1-1 in Germany.

'We always seem to get drawn against France,' said Houghton on the draw.

'We play them a lot and they are a very talented side and have one of the best teams in the world. We'd have preferred to play them last in the group stages and get some wins under our belt. We didn't know too much about Colombia and Mexico, but we didn't take them lightly.'

England would play their first two games in the little-known area of Moncton, before concluding their group in Montreal against the Colombians.

There was just the small matter for Sampson of selecting his squad, which was named at the Canadian Embassy in London on 11 May, less than a month before England began on their road to the final in Vancouver.

In were the likes of the previously overlooked Sanderson, and forward Jodie Taylor, who had never received a call-up from Powell despite a consistent scoring record playing in England, Australia, Sweden and America.

Also included, was a player Sampson would go on to describe as his 'mini Messi', a reference that would stick well after the World Cup. Fran Kirby was seen as somewhat of a wildcard for England. She was playing in England's second tier, The FA Women's Super League 2, but had shown over a period of time that she had all the attributes to be an international forward.

Sampson had given Kirby her debut in the team during the summer before he announced his squad in a friendly against Sweden. England won the game 4-0, and Kirby scored and impressed during the match.

That performance, along with her form with her club, gave the England coach no hesitation in selecting the twenty-one-year-old, for what would be her first senior tournament.

But while Kirby may have been somewhat of an unknown to those outside of England, Sampson had a squad of players that had benefited from the formation and expansion of the FA Women's Super League, the country's domestic competition, and continued investment from some of the league's bigger clubs – with Manchester City the latest to throw their weight behind their women's side after they went from amateur status to professional in 2014.

While benefiting from that extra investment and resource, Sampson would, for arguably the first time, be under the spotlight and his coaching credentials put to the test in his side's opening match with France.

His approach was different from that of Powell's. He was more laid back with his players and gave them more freedom when not in meetings or on the training field. But preparation was key, and captain Houghton outlined the work he did to ensure they were ready for all-comers.

'I think that's something we worked really hard on, on how we would structure our week in the lead up to a game.

'Everybody knew what Match Day minus-2 would look like, Match Day minus-1 and Match Day. To be honest, we had a lot of meetings, but at the time the group needed that, to be provided with information. The general theme was we'd look at the opposition, we'd look at the key players, we'd look at what the country was about and how they are perceived, strengths and weaknesses. Then the next day it would be about our game plan. Individually you know your role. You know your key influences. You know what your job is and that builds team togetherness.'

Despite Sampson's differing approach to that of Powell, and having an England squad available that was the most talented going into a World Cup, the opening game did not go according to plan, and the result was no different to that achieved under previous coach, Powell.

England suffered a 1-0 defeat in Moncton to France, courtesy of a goal from Lyon striker, Eugénie Le Sommer, in a match that Sampson's side rarely threatened, and looked to contain their opponents, rather than attack them.

The Welsh Head Coach came under scrutiny for the way he lined up his side in the match, which saw him deploy right-back Lucy Bronze at left-midfield to support left-back Claire Rafferty to try and nullify the threat of France's pacey right-winger, Elodie Thomis.

This was Sampson's first real test in a competitive match against an elite side, and his team had limped to a defeat that raised more questions than answers. The important thing now was to regroup and gain a positive result against Mexico.

That game would come four days later, and when not training or having meetings, England's players were limited in terms of entertainment in Moncton. The selection of the city raised eyebrows when announced as one of the host venues, especially since Toronto, a city with a men's Major League Soccer team, was controversially overlooked for selection due to the Pan American Games taking place in July.

'It was boring,' said Houghton, describing Moncton. 'We had two games there. I think we were there nine days, and the place was literally one street with a Starbucks and some restaurants on it. People tended to just walk around. There was a shopping mall about ten minutes away so people would go to the cinema or go for a walk just to break the day up.

'Although in the past I don't think we'd have been able to do that and would have been stuck in the hotel, so just to be able to get out a bit and see your friends and family or go out with the girls in your normal clothes, was great. But by the end of the Mexico game we got to the point where we needed to get out of that city.'

England would win that game against Mexico 2-1 thanks to Fran Kirby and Karen Carney, and it would be a special occasion for Reading striker Kirby, as she would start and score in the match, repaying the faith Sampson had shown by not only taking her to Canada, but by giving her a starting role.

It was a moment that Kirby will have savoured, because at one point in her career, it may never have happened. The young forward quit the game as a seventeen-year-old, three years after the death of her mother, and outlined just how much she struggled in an interview with the *Guardian*'s Anna Kessel.

'When I turned 17, that's when it all got a bit too much. I decided to stop doing pretty much everything. I quit football, I wouldn't get up in the morning, I wouldn't go out of my room, I was very depressed.'*

It was a special moment for Kirby, but she now, along with her teammates, would need to focus on the next game as they travelled to Montreal to face Colombia knowing that a win would see them progress to the knockout stages, which for the first time would see a round of sixteen stage after the expansion of the World Cup to twenty-four teams.

Carney was on the scoresheet again, and Fara Williams converted a penalty in another 2-1 win for England, who for the second game in a row, had frustratingly conceded in injury time to make the last few moments of the match nervier than they should have been.

But that didn't matter. England were through, and they would face a talented Norway side in the last sixteen after they finished runners-up in their group to Germany.

A win, and it would mean history for England, who had never been able to win a knockout match at a World Cup in 1995, 2007 or 2011. They had been knocked out at the quarter-final stage to Germany, the US and France respectively.

Ottawa, the scene of the World Cup draw, would play host to England and Norway, and after a disjointed first half, England would fall behind to a goal from Solveig Gulbrandsen just after half-time, which came as no surprise following a below-par first half.

'We didn't play well the first half against Norway,' said Houghton. 'It was so hot on a 3G pitch, it's burning your feet. It's a lot of pressure because it's the first time we could win a knockout game. We didn't get a hold of the game and we managed to get in 0-0. We needed to stop them playing and be aggressive, go through the things we went through in the week. It was a bit too like basketball,

---

* https://www.theguardian.com/football/2014/dec/27/england-forward
-fran-kirby-aiming-for-greatness-at-womens-world-cup

end to end. It was tough in that heat and we needed to get back to basics. But then it wasn't a great start to the second half because we conceded off a corner. I think at that moment you think "come on girls", then we started to get a grip of the game and started to get a few more corners.'

Those corners would soon pay off, as Houghton levelled seven minutes after Norway's opener thanks to a header from a Fara Williams cross.

'It's funny, the goal I scored, because we practised that a lot the day before in terms of runs and delivery. Set pieces were massive for us at that World Cup, and thankfully for me I timed my run well and I think I knocked Lucy Bronze over in the process. I think I had it in my head that I was beating my defender and it was going in. You don't even think you've scored in a World Cup, you're just thinking we need to get the next one.'

England did get the next one, and it came from a player who was starting to make a name for herself, Lucy Bronze. Widely considered one of the best right-backs in Europe, she was now starting to show what she could do on the world stage. Her defensive qualities were without question, but it was going forward that she was posing an equal threat. She showed her scoring ability when she belted in a 20-yard effort just twelve minutes from time to give England a 2-1 lead.

That goal would prove to be the winner, and for the first time at a World Cup, England had won a knockout match and their reward would be a quarter-final against hosts Canada in Vancouver.

The match would have added spice with Canada being coached by Newcastle born John Herdman, who as outlined earlier in this chapter, had been linked with the England job before Sampson's appointment.

Both coaches had a swagger about them, an arrogance that rubbed some people the wrong way. But that approach had helped their respective sides to a quarter-final, and it would be played in front of a crowd of fifty-four thousand fans – with the vast majority hoping for the hosts to progress.

For England's players, it would be walking out to a cauldron of noise that some of them, such as Kirby, would never have played in front of before.

The Canadian media and public were behind their team, but interest was also building back home in England, and Houghton admitted that with so much attention on the match, there were definitely nerves.

'We were excited, but we were nervous because there were fifty-four thousand Canadians who wanted us to get beat.

'There had been stuff in the press between the two managers and there's always been a bit of a rivalry from playing each other at the Cyprus Cup. I think it was the first time I had been to a stadium where I couldn't hear myself think. When we walked out you saw so many people and they were booing you every time you touched the ball, and that was surreal. But that spurred us on because you see that nobody wants you to win and you want to prove them wrong. Then you have the mentality that you won't be beaten.'

The match marked a first World Cup start for Jodie Taylor, who had come into the tournament carrying an injury and was only able to make substitute appearances in three of the previous matches.

Sampson had a lot of faith in the Portland Thorns striker, with her ability to hold up the ball and bring her midfielders into play. Starting her would prove to be a smart call, as it was she who would give England the lead on eleven minutes, after capitalising on an error from defender Lauren Sesselmann to fire past goalkeeper, Erin McLeod.

Three minutes later, it was two, and it was Lucy Bronze again as another England set-piece produced a positive outcome. The England right-back was able to ghost in at the back post to meet a long Fara Williams free-kick with a header, with the ball hitting the underside of the bar and beating McLeod. Suddenly, fifty-four thousand fans had been stunned into silence, and you could now hear a pin drop.

Canada's star forward Christine Sinclair scored just before half-time to halve the deficit, but England were in charge and worthy of their lead. However, their task would be made more difficult when they lost keeper Karen Bardsley to a bizarre injury. Crumb from the 3G pitch appeared to get into Bardsley's eye, causing it to swell. With her vision disrupted, Siobhan Chamberlain would replace her to make her World Cup debut.

Thankfully, Chamberlain was a safe pair of hands and an experienced head, and along with her teammates, was able to see out late Canada pressure to help her side achieve an historic victory, which meant a first World Cup semi-final for England's women's team, and they had done it by knocking out the hosts.

'For me, that win was my fondest memory of the World Cup,' said Houghton.

The prize for knocking out the hosts, was a contest against world champions, Japan: a team England were familiar with, having played them during the group stages of the 2007 and 2011 World Cups, beating them in 2011, before they went on to become the first Asian side to win a World Cup.

The match would be played in Edmonton and interest back in England was increasing, despite the time difference and late kick-off times. An audience of 1.7 million (peaking at 2.4 million) would tune in to watch England try and reach their first World Cup Final, but in their way was a Japan side with some of the world's most gifted players, with eight of the starting XI against England having played in the World Cup Final win over the United States in Frankfurt.[*]

[*] https://www.bbc.co.uk/sport/football/33404363

England, despite being underdogs, started the semi-final the much brighter of the two teams, and pressed the Japanese high up the field to try and counter their possession-based style. But despite that early pressure, it was Japan who would go ahead just after the half-hour mark when left-back Claire Rafferty was caught out of position and pushed Saori Ariyoshi in the box to give Japan a penalty. Captain Aya Miyama, who scored twice against England at the 2007 World Cup, coolly slotted home.

England responded magnificently, and just seven minutes later earned a penalty of their own. Yuki Ogimi, once of Chelsea, caught the heel of captain Houghton in the box, and Fara Williams, so reliable from the spot, converted to level.

England arguably deserved more going into the break. But Japan, with their vast experience of matches at this stage of a major tournament, were still very much in it.

The second half saw both teams create chances, with little to separate them as the game entered the last half an hour – you could cut the tension with a knife.

Then, just after the sixty-minute mark, England mounted an attack, with the ball falling to forward Toni Duggan on the edge of the box. She pinged an effort towards goal, but was met with the frustrating sound of leather colliding with metal as the ball cannoned off the bar.

Fine margins can settle games, and that matter of inches would contribute to one of the most heartbreaking moments witnessed in sport – men or women's.

In the ninety-second minute, Japan pushed forward down the right-hand side in search of a late winner. Nahomi Kawasumi found enough space to cross a dangerous ball into the box, but it wasn't met by a Japanese player. England defender Laura Bassett, who had been a rock throughout the tournament alongside Houghton, stuck out a leg and diverted the ball past Bardsley.

For the next few seconds, time seemed to stand still. For the thousands in the stadium, and the millions watching at home, what they had just witnessed felt like something out of a movie. Japan had scored with virtually the last kick of the game, and Bassett, along with some of her teammates, was inconsolable.

'I haven't spoken too much about that moment,' said Houghton. 'I don't remember a lot about it. I know the Japan game was one of our best performances. We pressed them high, Bass [Bassett] and my position were on the halfway line most of the time. We created chances. We were in the game throughout.

'Hindsight is a wonderful thing and I look back and think we could have managed the game better. We had a chance just before they scored. You think maybe you'll get another one. You think, "Could I have done this better, could I have done that better?" but when you play teams like Japan, they capitalise on mistakes, and they capitalise on the chances they get. You couldn't fault any of us on the pitch that day. The way we played and the emotions we went through to keep yourself prepared after five games is tough, but I think we were ready for that game, it just didn't seem to happen for us.'

The final whistle blew, and as captain, Houghton's role, along with that of Sampson, was to immediately console those around her.

But what about the captain herself? Was she able to show the same emotion as the other players because of that added responsibility?

'Your first reaction is this can't be happening; that's a natural reaction,' she said.

'At the end of the game you do the respectful thing of shaking the opposition's hands and the referee's hand, but deep down you're devastated. We were so close, one game from being in a World Cup Final. You go to see Bass to make sure she doesn't take it on herself, because she was unbelievable that tournament. I think in that moment I sat on the floor and had to take it all in. Of course you're upset because that's natural. I remember doing an interview straight after and remember having to pull myself together, because it's important in that moment that you have the right words to say. Not only show your emotion, but that a few days later you're playing a bronze-medal match.'

That must be tough?

'Yeah of course. It's not fake and I don't want to come across as fake. The day after you have to get your head back on. But I believed in that team and we still had a lot to achieve. But I won't lie, there was nobody speaking in the changing room after. But in that moment, I was like "come on girls, we've gone further than anyone expected us to or thought we would, we have a chance to win a medal." You just have to find the strength and energy to get around people, but also have that moment for yourself.

'I didn't sleep a wink that night, nobody did. There were a lot of tired faces the next morning and you play it over. You try not to look at your phone because you're getting lots of messages. Mark gave us the day off, no cool down, no reviews. In that moment in time, especially for Bass, to go off and do what she needed to do, it was important to have that time with family and switch off from football.'

England wouldn't be able to switch off for long, as after that much needed day off, it was time to regroup and prepare for a crunch third-place match against Germany – a side they had never beaten.

Attitudes towards bronze-medal matches are much different in the women's game to that of the men's. They matter, they mean something and England were never going to take the match lightly, despite some seeing it as a meaningless consolation.

The goal, according to Houghton, wasn't just to bring a medal home, but to make the country proud.

'I loved the fact that Mark [Sampson] said we have a new focus now, and that focus is to go and win a medal and we want to make the country proud. The biggest thing we wanted from the tournament was to inspire a nation and to inspire young girls to want to play football and watch us on TV.

'It was tough, but the chance of playing Germany and beating them for the first time to win a medal, coupled with all the support back home, you think, "we owe them one here".

'Then you look at how hard the Japan defeat was taken by Bass and some other individuals, and you want to feel like you owe them, I wanted to win a bronze for Bass to make her smile, even if it's just for that day, and to make the whole group smile.'

England would finish their World Cup journey in Edmonton against a side who had suffered a more straightforward defeat to the US by two goals to nil.

Germany's Silvia Neid, lauded as one of the game's greatest ever coaches, would present a stern test for Sampson, who had answered a lot of his critics, but was still yet to taste a win over what could be described as one of the world's superpowers in a competitive match.

Sampson had sprung somewhat of a surprise when he changed his formation to play three centre-backs, with Birmingham City's Jo Potter slotting in alongside Houghton and Bassett – the latter receiving a roar of approval on her name being read over the tannoy before the match. Whether English, German or neutral, everyone in the stadium knew the character it took Bassett to step onto that field that day.

England had been outplayed and outclassed less than a year before against the Germans when they lost 3-0 at Wembley, and Sampson's tactical reshuffle looked to ensure his side was more defensively robust.

The game in Edmonton was as expected, a tough one for England, and they were fortunate to have a goalkeeper – in Karen

Bardsley – in inspired form. She made a string of fine saves in the first half, while Houghton also flung herself at a goal-bound effort that she hooked off the line. England were under pressure, but they were still in the match.

The second half played out similar to the first, but England stood firm despite Germany's perseverance, and the match would go into extra-time.

Attacking midfielder Lianne Sanderson had been brought on ten minutes before the match went into extra-time, and she would play a key part in England breaking the deadlock and grabbing the advantage.

Three minutes into the second period of extra-time and twelve minutes before a dreaded penalty shoot-out, Sanderson found some space in the box and was being hustled by left-back, Tabea Kemme. But the German defender got too tight to Sanderson, and wrapped her arms around the Arsenal attacker to prevent her progress. The referee spotted the foul, blew the whistle, and England had a penalty.

Fara Williams, much like she had done in the group stage, stepped up and slotted past German number one Nadine Angerer, herself a two-time World Cup winner, to give England a priceless lead.

Despite late pressure from Germany, England stood firm, and for the first time in the country's history, they had won a bronze medal and achieved England's best finish at a senior World Cup since the men's 4-2 win over Germany in 1966.

In the space of a few days, England's players had gone from experiencing the lowest of lows, to the highest of highs. They had won a medal. They had beaten Germany. And they had done it just days after suffering the lowest point of their career. It took courage, bravery and heart. All characteristics of a Lioness, you could say.

Above all, England had ended their tournament in the best way possible – celebrating.

'It was an emotional rollercoaster,' said Houghton.

'We got the penalty and you wouldn't ask anyone else but Fara to take that. After the game we were so tired, and we'd had so many emotions throughout that tournament, it was relief, but at the same time, we were so delighted.

'We celebrated in the changing rooms a little bit, but it was all about getting back to the hotel as all the family went back. We had a quick meeting where players presented a shirt to the staff. Everyone was downstairs at the bar having a few drinks. There were a few songs being sang, a few sore heads the next morning and then two flights to catch back, which wasn't very good.'

What was very good was the reception the team received when they got home. Fans and media were waiting at Heathrow airport to greet their Lionesses, who had gone to the World Cup and inspired a new generation of fans, while also propelling England into the elite teams of women's football.

The team was invited to be guests at Wimbledon just days after arriving back, while they were also invited to meet with Prince William.

Houghton admitted that despite the desperate loss to Japan in the semi-final, the reception when they arrived home made her realise just how special a tournament it had been.

'I think the messages and the media attention, not just for us as individuals but the game at home, was massive. People began to respect us as footballers, and not just see us as girls that play football. I think we were very lucky to be invited to meet Prince William, that's what comes with success. You do have a smile to yourself because you've achieved so much.'

Around 2.4 million people had tuned in to watch England finish third at the World Cup, as numbers of viewers gradually increased throughout the tournament.*

* https://www.theguardian.com/commentisfree/2017/aug/07/tv-

England's Lionesses were now respected, admired, and most importantly, they were seen as a force in world football. With that success, comes interest, and while the domestic game continues to struggle to attract large numbers, the Lionesses saw an even bigger TV audience tune in for their EURO 2017 quarter-final win over France (3.3 million) with four million tuning in to their semi-final defeat to the Netherlands.*

Journalist Tony Leighton, who covered England's journey to bronze in 2015 and followed England for more than twenty years, said belief and confidence instilled into the team by Sampson was key to their success, and played a part in England subsequently going on to become one of the world's best.

'He got the players believing in each other, and believing in themselves.

'There were young players in that squad who had no fear. They felt they could go onto that stage and perform. Then you had players like Casey Stoney, knowing that she wouldn't get many minutes, but she played a really important role.

'This was the fittest England team and best organised I had seen in all my time covering them. They were full of confidence, and that's why they were able to achieve what they did, inspire so many people, and really live up to their Lionesses tag.'

audience-england-womens-football-lionesses
* https://www.theguardian.com/media/2017/aug/04/englands-lion-esses-smash-tv-audience-record-euro-2017-semi-final-women-football

Marta's Time to Shine

....

No sport is immune to the conversation about the G.O.A.T. – the greatest of all time. Debate will forever rage over which player was the best to ever grace her respective arena of play, a charming yet infuriating conversation which captures the essence of sports fandom. It's difficult to remove generational or geographical biases, and it's typically impossible to compare such players directly, since the scarcity of them often means their careers don't directly overlap.

Women's soccer's G.O.A.T. conversation is slightly simpler – but only slightly – given the relatively short history of the modern, sanctioned era. The United States' Michelle Akers, and China's Sun Wen, in 2000 were named by FIFA as co-players of the century. Sun Wen's name is often lost in the wider conversation about the best to play the sport, and in the US, the conversation often boils down to a three-American debate: Michelle Akers, Mia Hamm or Abby Wambach. Akers is the common pick among the purists, an irreplaceable player who won a Women's World Cup title as a holding midfielder ten years after she won a World cup as a target forward. That is special.

The G.O.A.T. conversation is largely rooted in a basic comparative: Who is better? Hamm and Akers played together but were completely different players; Sun Wen played during their era. Akers and Wambach share many characteristics, but their careers never overlapped.

Different from all these players is Marta, the Brazilian who burst onto the scene as a teenager in the 2000s and redefined greatness in women's soccer. Marta has been voted the world's best player on

45

six different occasions, including five straight from 2006 to 2010. Her mesmerising abilities with the ball at her feet are the epitome of the Brazilian *ginga* style of play; the crafty, precise, entertaining – and, truly, showboating – style of play which makes Brazilian players so distinguishable.

This sort of beautiful, free-flowing soccer is the root of all of Brazil's success in the sport – on the men's side. And while entertaining female Brazilian players came before Marta – Sissi and Katia among them – nobody captured the public eye like Marta.

She first appeared on international radars as a seventeen-year-old at the 2003 Women's World Cup in the United States, scoring fourteen minutes into an opening-match victory over South Korea. She scored again in Brazil's second match, a 4-1 victory over Norway, and she would play every minute for Brazil, who lost to Sweden in the quarter-finals. Marta attempted and converted the penalty kick which briefly drew Brazil level in that match. That she was given that responsibility – and that she was wearing the iconic number ten jersey in canary yellow as a teenager – was a testament to the promise she held. She hadn't quite taken over the 2003 World Cup, but she displayed a rare set of exquisite skills and she oozed confidence. Still a teenager, her potential was enormous. *Who is this kid?* At least one club was serious about finding out.

Roland Arnqvist, then manager of Swedish club Umeå IK, knew that he was looking at the future of the sport. Umeå, through a Portuguese interpreter, began to aggressively recruit the teenage Brazilian, who initially needed some convincing that they were serious. She thought it was a joke.

Marta signed with the club and arrived in Sweden for the first time in February 2004. A group of journalists welcomed her to her new, snowy surroundings in what had the look of an impromptu outdoor press conference. She had no idea what she was in for – nor how much her life was about to change.

'The beginning was really hard,' Marta said in a 2011 ESPN documentary. 'Communicating was tough. The cold was, too. I couldn't feel my feet. It was a big challenge, but I just focused on soccer.'

Marta grew up in Dois Riachos in the Alagoas state of Brazil, an impoverished area in the northeast of the country which largely relies on agriculture to survive. She was one of four kids to a single mother, and from an early age, she was different – she was a girl who loved to play football. She was subject to degrading comments simply for loving a sport – a sport which she was exceptional at – and for playing with boys' teams, which were her only options. That is, until they weren't. Marta would later recount a time when she was removed from a regional tournament because a coach from another team said he would pull his team. Instead, as Marta recalls, she left in order for her team to continue playing.*

She left not just a team, but her home. Marta, with no guarantees, got on a bus and travelled for three days to Rio de Janeiro for the chance to try out for the women's team at Vasco da Gama, a century-old club on the men's side. Her trek, which she made thanks to the support of friends, was only for the possibility of a tryout.

A cousin and a couple of close friends helped Marta get out of her small town. They knew that Marta could be something special and that if she was going to thrive, she would need more than Dois Riachos could offer. She was going to need boots that fitted her, not hand-me-downs she could only fit in by stuffing them with newspapers. She was going to need a real ball and a real field, not the dirt roads which defined her rural area. She was going to need an actual women's team to escape the shadow and spectacle of being *that girl*

* https://www.theplayerstribune.com/en-us/articles/marta-brazil-letter-to-my-younger-self

on the boys' team and perhaps rise to the national team. She was going to need help.

As Marta recalls in her 2018 'Letter to My Younger Self' on The Players' Tribune, she waited days before the phone call came for that tryout. When she finally got her opportunity, she was amazed by the sight she had yet to see in her young life: a field full of women playing football.

She was shy then, as she remains today. The scene was intimidating: Vasco da Gama's senior team and its U19 squad out on the pitch practising. Here she was, at age 14, the 'bicho do mato' – the hick from the backwoods – as she recalls being dubbed. With little to say in return, she did what she knows best; she let her play do the talking.

> And when you step onto the field, your first touch will be a kick so hard that it knocks the goalkeeper on her back when she tries to stop it.
>
> And the ball will roll into the goal.
>
> Heads will turn towards you. But the stares won't be for the same reasons back at home. They won't be staring at you wondering, Why are you here?
>
> No, this time they'll be wondering, Are you for real?
>
> And then someone will finally speak. It'll be Helena Pacheco, the coordinator of the women's senior side.
>
> 'We want her with us.'
>
> With us.*

Marta progressed from Vasco da Gama, which would soon shutter its women's team, to the international stage, first at the U-19 World Cup in 2002 and then at the senior level a year later.

* https://www.theplayerstribune.com/en-us/articles/marta-brazil-letter-to-my-younger-self

Her move to Sweden to play professionally would shape not just the rest of her soccer career, but her entire life. She began her journey as a wide-eyed teenager in a foreign place – a place which treated women's football seriously. Sweden would become her second home. She would score about a goal per game for Umeå – a practically unheard of rate – in her four years there before heading to the United States in 2009 to become the reluctant face of the new US pro league. By that point, she was a superstar.

First, however, she had another World Cup to contend.

Brazil opened their 2007 Women's World Cup campaign with a 5-0 route over an overwhelmed New Zealand side. Marta scored twice on a pair of emphatic finishes which brought a roar from the crowd of over fifty thousand in Wuhan, China. The home fans were entertained. Marta was magic – and she was just warming up.

Three days later, in front of fifty-four thousand fans at that same venue, she and fellow rising star Cristiane would punish the hosts, 4-0. Marta and Cristiane each scored twice. A late goal from Pretinha against Denmark sent the Brazilians through to the knockout stage with a perfect record. They held on in the quarter-finals to beat a plucky, upstart Australian team, 3-2. Marta scored from the penalty spot for her fifth goal of the tournament, and Cristiane scored a magnificent game-winner, turning and firing a shot from 20 yards out while surrounded by six Australian defenders. Brazil had a duo for the future.

Now standing in the way of *Seleção* and the World Cup final were their rivals and two-time world champions, the Americans.

American history tells the story of that 27 September 2007 semifinal in Hangzhou as one of the all-time meltdowns. Goalkeeper Hope Solo had started each of the first four matches of the tournament for the United States heading into that semi-final and there was no question that she was the starter; she had been for about two years. She hadn't given up a goal in the preceding three matches heading into the semi-final, and the US appeared to be humming along in the World Cup, as they always did.

That's when then-US Head Coach Greg Ryan benched Solo in favour of Briana Scurry, the 1999 World Cup hero who had that month turned thirty-six years old. It was a bizarre decision that would soon lead to the end of Ryan's tenure in charge and to a divided US locker room which needed repairing before a return to China for the 2008 Olympics. Solo would call out Ryan on international television after the United States' 4-0 loss: 'I think it was the wrong decision. And I think anybody that knows anything about the game knows that. There's no doubt in my mind I would have made those saves.' Solo was then ostracised from the team as it practised for and won the third-place match.

Of course, that is the American side of what happened that night in China. It has been well detailed and it served to overshadow the brilliance that was Marta.

The US fell behind twenty minutes into the match on an own goal from Leslie Osborne, who misjudged a corner kick and headed the ball into her own net. The home crowd erupted for Brazil. Seven minutes later, Marta doubled Brazil's lead, collecting the ball on the sideline, cutting inside to her favoured left foot and eluding three defenders before firing a low shot from 17 yards out. Scurry reacted slowly – further fuelling the team's self-created goalkeeper controversy – and could only push the ball into the net. Brazil led 2-0, and the US was in trouble. The goal was Marta's sixth of the tournament.

Marta continued to give hell to the Americans. She was the quickest player on the field with and without the ball. Every touch of the ball brought more confidence to Marta and her teammates. With each touch, it seemed clear that Marta was closer to scoring again than the US was to stopping her. With each successful Brazilian foray forward, the crowd of nearly forty-eight thousand fans grew a little louder. An anticipatory crescendo of crowd noise came with each cross and each shot. Brazil was feeling it.

And Marta kept on dancing. In the seventy-eighth minute, with the Brazilians comfortably controlling the match, she would spin-turn on the endline, pulling the ball back and then pushing it forward to elude her defender all while tight-walking the line in one, fluid motion. This was Samba with a ball. This was Marta, a once-in-a-lifetime player. This was *ginga* – and that wasn't the Americans' style.

'Look at the magic!' ESPN broadcaster J. P. Dellacamera yells. 'Put all of Marta's moves right there on a highlight video,' he continues. He was slightly ahead of the times. The social media era of snackable content and viral videos was nearly upon us, and Marta was to be its posterchild for women's soccer.

'The ball is like glue to her foot!' former US international and ESPN analyst Julie Foudy says as the world feed shows a replay of the move.

'There is no woman player that can do any of this,' Dellacamera exclaims.

A dubious second yellow card for Shannon Boxx on the verge of half-time had reduced the US to ten players, and the uphill task became monumental. Brazil was toying with them now, a completely unfamiliar position for the Americans. Cristiane had scored Brazil's third goal eleven minutes after half-time and proceeded actually to dance in celebration. The United States' fifty-one-match unbeaten streak was clearly about to implode in spectacular fashion, but not without one more trick from the world's best player.

One minute after her wonderful spin-turn displaced US defender Tina Frimpong, the two were matched up once again. With her back to the US goal, Marta trapped a bouncing pass with her right foot. Her touch, to the naked eye, looked subpar – the ball bounced up on her. But before it returned to the ground, she swung her left leg backward, flicking the ball around the left side of Frimpong as she simultaneously ran around the American's right shoulder. She sold a fake shot – no player in history can fake out a defender using her hips the way Marta can – and sent US defender Cat Whitehill sprawling before cutting back inside to her right foot to bury her shot from 10 yards out. It remains among the most memorable and spectacular goals in Women's World Cup history.

Marta had arrived.

'I played in a way that was really special,' she said years later. 'I can say it's the most beautiful goal I've ever scored.

'I see this as the best moment not only for me but the whole Brazilian team during the World Cup. It was very exciting, and this game made history.'[*]

Brazil would lose to Germany, 2-0, in the final – a match which saw German goalkeeper Nadine Angerer deny Marta a would-be equaliser from the penalty spot. It was a disappointing end to the tournament for Brazil, losers of a major tournament final for the second straight time after falling to the US in the 2004 Olympics.

Marta's mark on the tournament was felt. She won the Golden Boot as top scorer with seven goals, and she was awarded the Golden Ball as the tournament's best player. Two months later, she would be named the world's best player again.

What was made clear in that tournament – and, in particular, by that otherworldly flick-to-self-goal against the US – is that this was a player unlike any the game had seen before.

Away from the field, Marta is a shy and private person. She has lived most of her life in the awkward fringes of anonymity and celebrity

[*] https://www.youtube.com/watch?v=YLAFL4219PU

that comes with life as a women's soccer star. A men's player of her pedigree would have no privacy, but the still-fledgling state of the women's game allows Marta to live on the right side of the paparazzi pH scale, closer to the way she'd prefer.

Brazil has come around on recognising Marta's achievements in recent years, but the federation's longstanding neglect for and lack of investment in its women's programme remains one of the all-time 'What if?' questions. How many World Cup and Olympic titles could Brazil's women's team have won if they had even been afforded the slightest bit more support from the federation? As of 2018, they have still yet to appear on the top step of a podium at a major tournament.

Marta had to leave. Staying in Brazil, where women's soccer is still so far behind the men's game, wasn't an option.

'Football is a religion here, but this country has not been there for Marta: She'd never be recognised as one of the best players in the world if she had stayed in Brazil,' Marta's longtime agent, Fabiano Farah, told *The Globe and Mail* during the 2015 World Cup. 'Who's the most awarded football player in the world? It's a woman – but that answer is a bit awkward in Brazil.'*

Marta remains a proud Brazilian and now, a Swedish citizen, as well. Both places are home for her. She would return to Sweden to play for two different clubs from 2012 to 2017 before a move back to the US to join the Orlando Pride of the National Women's Soccer League. And her incredible form for club and country continues.

The 2011 and 2015 World Cups were unkind to Brazil, who lost their first knockout-round match in both editions of the tournament. At the conclusion of the 2015 Women's World Cup – Marta's fourth – her fifteen goals stood as the all-time record. A near-run of

* https://www.theglobeandmail.com/sports/soccer/a-vicious-circle-plagues-the-world-of-womens-soccer-in-brazil/article24954058/

destiny on home soil at the 2016 Rio Summer Olympics ended in further heartbreak – a fourth-place finish, missing the podium entirely.

Marta has, at times in her six world's-best acceptance speeches and through various other platforms, deflected individual praise and tried to shine the spotlight on her teammates. She has spoken of her desire to trade the individual trophies for championships. No greater opportunity for that existed than in 2007. Brazil's best Women's World Cup team ever fell just short. Individual accolades might be small consolations for Marta, but in 2007, she laid down a marker in the G.O.A.T. conversation. She sent notice to the world and to her country: it didn't matter that she was a woman – she was as special a soccer player as the planet was ever going to see.

Dois Riachos remains a humble place, but its citizens have long beamed with pride over the one who left to chase greatness. Turn off highway BR-316 to head into the centre of town and you'll drive under a sign which stretches across the roadway. Overhead it welcomes you to the home of Marta:

BEM VINDO A DOIS RIACHOS
TERRA DA JOGADORA MARTA

On the supporting pillar to the left is a photo of the town's hero. Under her name, the sign reads: 'A MELHOR JOGADORA DE FUTEBOL DO MUNDO'

Translation: 'THE BEST SOCCER PLAYER IN THE WORLD'

The Germans
Own the Decade

....

Former England international and now broadcaster Gary Lineker once famously used the line, 'Football is a simple game. Twenty-two men chase a ball for 90 minutes and at the end, the Germans always win.'

Lineker was of course referring to the dominance of the German team that won the World Cup under Franz Beckenbauer at Italia 90. But replace the term 'men' with 'women', and he could quite easily have been talking about their female counterparts, who dominated the women's game in the 2000s, seeing off all before them to claim five tournament wins in nine years.

Amongst those triumphs, were the 2003 and 2007 World Cups, making Germany the only side in women's football history to claim back-to-back titles since the inaugural tournament in 1991.

This will come as little surprise to most, with the Germans having had the likes of the likes of Ariane Hingst, Birgit Prinz and Nadine Angerer, who were amongst an exceptionally talented group of players.

With the first World Cup held in 1991, Germany would have to wait twelve years to emulate the 1990 triumph of their male counterparts, with their best effort before their first World Cup triumph coming in 1995 when they lost out narrowly to Norway in the final in Stockholm. This was very much a tale of two strikers, with Norway led by Hege Riise, arguably Norway's greatest ever player and in the prime of her career, with Germany's front line led by a forward just starting out on her journey to greatness – a seventeen-year-old by the name of Birgit Prinz.

Norway's 2-0 triumph meant a first World Cup for the Scandinavians, and an unwanted silver for Germany's Head Coach Gero Bisanz. He had led the team to three triumphs in the Women's European Championships in 1989, 1991 and 1995, but was unable to take his side to the next level and cross the line at a World Cup.

Bisanz would lead the side for fourteen years between 1982 and 1996, which was no easy task as Germany had only overturned the ban on women playing football twelve years before he began his tenure.

Similar to other countries, like England, there was uncertainty surrounding women playing football, with clubs banned from having women's teams in the 1950s and '60s. It wasn't until October 1970 that the ban was lifted, meaning women's football in Germany would finally be recognised, but was playing catch up with some of the other nations who already had established women's teams.

As Bisanz looked to put a setup and structure in place in his early years, he would also have to oversee changes in the team due to the German reunification.

Having competed as West Germany since 1970, the team would participate in the first Women's World Cup in China as Germany, as by this point, West and East Germany had become one nation following the reunification on 3 October 1990.

Germany would finish fourth at the 1991 World Cup and would follow that up with a runners-up spot four years later at the tournament held in Sweden, after defeat in the final to Norway.

The Germans would have an opportunity to seek that elusive world title the following year in 1996, but it wouldn't come in the shape of the World Cup. Instead, for the first time, women's football would be represented at the Summer Olympics in Atlanta.

Those Olympics would prove memorable for Germany for very

different reasons, with the end of an era for one individual, and new beginnings for another.

Germany's third-place finish in their group meant elimination before the knockout stages, and resulted in Head Coach Bisanz resigning from his position after fourteen years in charge, believing that the team needed a fresh approach.

The then sixty-year-old had left a lasting legacy having been instrumental in the formation of the team, their three European Championships under his tenure, and the development of some of the country's greatest ever players – two of whom, Silvia Neid and Steffi Jones, would go on to coach the national team with very differing fortunes.

Bisanz died at the age of seventy-nine after suffering a sudden heart-attack in October 2014, which prompted the DFB (Germany's governing body for football) president Wolfgang Niersbach to say in a statement: 'The news of his sudden death has hit us all very hard at the DFB. Gero Bisanz was a wonderful person and true professional, who made a lasting contribution to football. By winning the European Championship in 1989, he helped women's football in Germany make its breakthrough in terms of public awareness and appreciation.'*

The trailblazing coach was replaced by his assistant, who had worked alongside him during his fourteen years in charge. Tina Theune had the unenviable task of trying to emulate the achievements of Bisanz, while also carving out her own legacy. Bringing in her own players and enforcing her own style of play would be one of the first tasks for Theune, who had seen the rise and progression of the national team under Bisanz, but now needed to create her own team identity.

* https://www.dfb.de/en/news/detail/dfb-mourns-the-loss-of-gero-bisanz-108369/?no_cache=1

One of those players that she brought in was defender, Ariane Hingst. She would go on to become one of Germany's most coveted players – receiving her first call-up from Theune at just seventeen and going on to work with her for nine years.

'Tina was neither a hand-round-the-shoulder or have-a-go-at-you coach,' said Hingst. 'She trusted us and she was very tactical. We had meeting after meeting after meeting, which could be a bit annoying, but she made sure we were ready for every opponent.'

As well as bringing in new players, Theune would have to deal with the loss of some of her experienced heads, and few came more experienced than Silvia Neid, who announced her retirement after the 1996 Olympics. Neid's influence would not be lost, however, as she would join Theune's coaching staff and coach some of the country's youth teams.

Germany's dominance of the European Championship continued when they retained their title in 1997 in a revamped competition that saw the tournament expanded to eight teams. Despite a defeat in the group stages to Norway, Germany would qualify out of their group and defeat Sweden in the semi-final, before a win over Italy in the final, thanks to goals from Sandra Minnert and Birgit Prinz.

That European title, Germany's fourth in eight years, was a sign of a growing dominance of women's football in their own continent.

But that search for a global title would continue as the Germans departed for the 1999 World Cup in America for Theune's first tournament in charge outside of Europe. While the Germans were disappointing during the competition, suffering elimination at the quarter-final stage, the experience in the US would prove a nice warm up, unexpectedly, for what would soon come their way.

After the disappointment of the 1999 World Cup, Germany would win bronze at the Sydney Olympics in 2000 – the first football Olympic medal for Germany since the men won a bronze in

Seoul in 1988 – before claiming yet another European title a year later back home in Germany.

The 2001 tournament will be remembered for being the first European final that was settled by a Golden Goal. After opening the tournament against Sweden in front of ten thousand fans, Germany would cruise past England and Russia to reach the knockout phase of the competition, beating rivals Norway in the semi-final.

That meant a final against Sweden – the team they had opened against – in Ulm, situated on the River Danube.

Treacherous weather made for a difficult game for both sides, which inevitably saw the game end goalless and go into extra-time. The historic Golden Goal that separated the two sides came from Claudia Müller eight minutes into the first-half of extra-time, handing Germany their fifth European title in front of a crowd of over eighteen thousand fans.

The question now, having won three European titles in a row, and five of the last six, was could they transfer that form into a World Cup?

What would develop over the next six years between 2001 and 2007 would answer that question and put any doubt that Germany could be a world champion, well and truly to bed.

The battle to host the 2003 World Cup came down to two nations, China and Australia – two countries with vastly different backgrounds in the women's game, with the Chinese having just lost the final of the 1999 World Cup to the US, and Australia having never won a match at FIFA's showpiece tournament.

In October 2000, Australian football federation president Basil Scarsella revealed that FIFA had decided to award the competition to China, saying: 'We have no doubt that China will hold an excellent event but we believe, after the success of the Olympic Soccer (at the Sydney Olympics), that we would have done it better.'

It would be the first Women's World Cup held in Asia with the previous tournaments having been held in North America and Europe, and would give FIFA Golden Ball winner from 1999, Sun Wen, the opportunity to showcase her talents to a home audience.

For Tina Theune and her side, their first objective was to lay to rest the demons of their quarter-final exit in 1999, and top their UEFA qualification group to secure their place in China.

As with any nation, the squad evolved, and the makeup of Theune's team had seen a number of changes from the squad that had turned out in the United States in 1999.

No longer could she call on the experience of defender Doris Fitschen, who had captained the side and was named in the 1999 World Cup All-Star team, due to retirement. Martina Voss, widely regarded alongside Fitschen as one of Germany's greats, would also not be available having retired before the European Championships in 2001.

But this opened the door to new players; players who would go on to have long careers with the national team. The likes of Turbine Potsdam's Conny Pohlers, who would spend a decade playing for her country, and Bad Neuenahr's Martina Müller, who was part of the 2001 EUROs side and would go on to win a century of caps, winning everything at club and international level.

The change in personnel also allowed for some of those who had been in and around the squad for a few years to step up to the mark and lead the team. Striker Birgit Prinz was one of those, and defender Hingst was another.

'We had seen change, but while those players were really important and contributed a lot, we knew we had a good team going into qualification for the 2003 World Cup, and we still had a lot of experienced players,' said Hingst.

She was right to be optimistic. Her side were drawn alongside England, Portugal and the Netherlands in their qualifying group, and they breezed past all of them, winning six matches out of six, scoring thirty goals at an average of five every match, and conceding just one.

Pohlers made an immediate impact, scoring five against Portugal in a 9-0 win, while Müller bagged a hat-trick in the same match.

Qualification ended where it had started, against England, with Theune's side running out narrow 1-0 winners to top the table comfortably, and book their plane ticket to China.

However, it wouldn't be China that they would be heading to – they would instead be re-booking a ticket back to the United States, scene of their quarter-final exit four years earlier.

In November 2002, there were reports in the Guangdong area of China of an outbreak of severe acute respiratory syndrome, more commonly referred to as SARS.

The disease spread over the following months to other areas, including Hong Kong, with the World Health Organisation (WHO) advising people not to travel to areas such as Hong Kong and the Guangdong Province in China.[*]

According to the Centers for Disease Control and Prevention, between November 2002 and May 2003, there were a total of 8,098 cases of SARS reported worldwide, with 774 people dying as a result of the disease.

Understandably, as a result, on 3 May 2003, FIFA took the decision to remove the Women's World Cup from China, with the compensation that the country would be able to host the next competition in 2007.[†]

With the tournament scheduled to start on 23 September, it didn't allow much time for a replacement to be found, or for that replacement to organise the tournament at such short notice.

* https://www.who.int/ith/diseases/sars/en/
† https://www.cdc.gov/about/history/sars/timeline.htm

Australia, who, as already outlined, had bid for the rights to host the tournament before losing out to China, now alongside the United States expressed an interest in hosting.

FIFA gave interested parties until 18 May to submit their bids to host the tournament, with the United States and Sweden being the two countries who formally registered their interest. Australia did not follow through with a bid. Canada also expressed an interest to host games in Edmonton, should the United States be successful with their application. Four days before a decision was made, Canada withdrew their interest.

On 23 May an emergency FIFA committee meeting was held in Zurich to discuss the two bids, with the United States officially awarded the tournament three days later.

'This is an historic day for soccer in the United States,' said US Soccer President Dr. S. Robert Contiguglia. 'We have been confident from the very beginning that our infrastructure and experience could make this a reality, and we now have approximately 120 days to do something that no one has ever attempted. Staging an event of this stature and size in this short amount of time will be a great challenge, but we will succeed because of the support and organizational abilities of the entire U.S. Soccer family.'*

The tournament had officially been moved, and Germany defender Hingst was not sorry to see it played outside of China.

'To be honest, we were glad the tournament was moved to the USA. Back then, there were no business class flights and it was an eleven-hour journey to China. The contract the German FA had with China meant we had to travel there every year, and we didn't enjoy playing there. It was tough conditions, very humid,

* https://www.ussoccer.com/stories/2014/03/17/13/58/2003-fifa-womens-world-cup-relocated-to-united-states

you didn't have your own chef back then and you didn't really want to go out. In the US we knew the climate; even the grass is different in China. You could go out and go and grab a coffee or something in the US, but China had smog, so you were less likely to go out.'

The draw for the tournament took place at the Home Depot Center in Carson, California, on 17 July, just two months before the tournament was due to commence. Germany were handed matches against Canada, Japan and Argentina.

The matches had been scheduled as doubleheaders, with Germany's group based in Columbus, Ohio for the first two matches, before the final Group C matches were paired with Group B, with Germany and Argentina travelling to Washington, D.C. to play a doubleheader alongside France and Brazil.

Staying focused going into the tournament was key, especially off the back of another European Championship victory. But when you have a character like goalkeeper Nadine Angerer in your squad going into a tournament, there is always someone there to help the team unwind and relax.

Angerer adopted the same role she had been allocated in the 1999 squad of being back-up to Theune's number one choice, Silke Rottenberg. As a second-choice keeper, you know that unless there is a dramatic drop in form, injury or suspension, you are unlikely to see time on the field, which is why, according to Angerer, you sometimes have to play a different role.

'I used to joke around a lot, I was the clown,' she said. 'Often players want to be in their zone, but I think it's always good to have a joke with them to keep them relaxed. I would hide stuff and played around with them. I think I annoyed some of them, but I didn't care because I wanted them to be relaxed and distracted from the big occasion. I was one of the younger players, but I had been in the national team for six or seven years.

'I went by myself and bought some DVDs and I opened a DVD store in my room so players could come to my room and they could rent my portable DVD player – it was just for fun, not money.

'I am an explorer so as soon as we arrived in the US, I put my suitcase in my room and explored the city. I found some crazy massage salons, tried it first and then told all the players of my experience.

'But we always had our door open and had good team spirit. There were no egos in our squad. I think that's why we were strong, we always had a very tight squad.'

Angerer may have been the clown in 2003, but her role would become more significant four years later, which is covered later in this chapter.

The Germans were ruthless throughout the group stages in 2003, dominating Canada in their opening match 4-1, with Prinz amongst the scorers as she set out on the road to becoming top scorer in the tournament.

Japan were then brushed aside thanks to a double from Prinz and a solitary effort from defender Sandra Minnert, before Theune's side travelled to Washington to thrash Argentina 6-1. Maren Meinert grabbed a brace, and Prinz added her fourth of the tournament.

A trip to Portland, Oregon for the quarter-final would follow to face Russia, who had finished runners-up to China during the group stages. On paper, it was an easy win for Germany, and that proved to be the case as Prinz made it six for the tournament with a double, while Kerstin Garefrekes also notched two in a 7-1 thumping of the Russians.

The win importantly meant no travel, with the semi-final scheduled in Portland, but it did mean a repeat of the 1999 quarter-final against the hosts, USA.

Both Angerer and Hingst complimented the winning mentality of the United States, and surprisingly agreed that the German mentality was more pessimistic – this despite their dominance of European football. Angerer confessed her side didn't necessarily have the strong winning mentality of their US counterparts.

'We are Germans, so we doubt everything, we don't have the self-confidence and are the opposite of the US,' said Angerer.

'The US is sometimes too optimistic, and we are sometimes too pessimistic, I don't know why, I think it's a cultural thing. Even if we win a World Cup, our first thought is what can we do better next time.'

Head Coach Theune will have thought of everything to remove that doubt from her team, especially coming up against a side that were at home, in front of 27,623 fans, and having the confidence of having beaten the Germans four years earlier.

But as Hingst explains, Theune was able to give her side a mental edge as they went out to warm up ahead of the contest, through the power of music.

'Tina played music that could be annoying, it wasn't my sort of thing. But she played this one song that we liked and it became a bit of a team song – it was by Nena Kerner and Kim Wilde called "Anyplace Anywhere Anytime". We went out to warm up for the semi-final against the USA, and then we stopped, because the song came on over the stadium speakers.

'Tina had managed to get them to play our song to the whole stadium – we knew after that we were not going to lose.'

That move by Theune had all of a sudden given her side a psychological boost. A smart move by a coach who, as outlined by goalkeeper Angerer, knew that her players would have had doubts of winning going into the match.

It would turn out to be a stroke of genius.

While the players still had to go onto the field and perform, the Germans had overcome their demons, and put in one of their best performances at a World Cup.

Coming up against the likes of Mia Hamm, Kristine Lilly and Brandi Chastain, who had so famously and so dramatically overcome China on penalties in front of ninety thousand spectators at the Los Angeles Rose Bowl four years earlier, was never going to be easy. But nerves were settled just fifteen minutes into the match, when Garefrekes met a Renate Lingor corner to flick a header past Briana Scurry in the US goal to score her fourth goal of the tournament.

Desperate defending followed at times for Germany, with Lilly and Hamm both going close, but there was no way through for the USA.

As the game went on, the hosts piled forward, which left space and opportunities for Germany to counter. As the crowd roared on their side in the dying minutes, Germany exploited that space to score twice in injury time. Prinz and Meinert were the players to do the damage. Meinert added Germany's second following a through ball from Prinz, before she returned the favour for her strike partner to grab her seventh goal of the tournament, while claiming another assist for herself – her seventh of the tournament.

Cue wild celebrations as the crowd, made up predominantly of Americans, were stunned into silence.

Germany had reached their second Women's World Cup fnal, and it would come against Sweden, the very country within which they had lost their first in Stockholm.

But they would not prepare for the match as you would expect. There were no intense training sessions, no long meetings, and no strict curfews. In fact, Theune gave her players some time off, as Ariane Hingst explains.

'After beating the USA, we just had this feeling that we're not going to lose, although we knew Sweden would be a difficult match.

'Tina said after the game, "I don't care what you do over the next seven days, but you are not going to be training. I just want you on that field next week ready for the final." It was a real show of trust in us. We met every morning at 10am for breakfast, and met on the field a few times because we wanted to be ready. We didn't do anything stupid the rest of the time, and we didn't take advantage of Tina's trust.'

The World Cup would come full circle with the final held in Carson, California, the same venue where the draw for the tournament had taken place less than three months earlier.

Only two years earlier had Germany and Sweden met in the final of the European Championships, and now they would square off again in front of twenty-six thousand fans – many of which would have been there expecting to see the USA.

The Swedes were led by Hanna Ljunberg and Victoria Svensson, who came into the final with five goals between them, and were widely considered two of Sweden's greats.

With the two sides closely matched over the years, it's no surprise that there was little to separate them in the final.

It took forty-one minutes for the deadlock to be broken, when the two Swedish stars combined, with Svensson sending Ljunberg through one-on-one with Rottenberg, before she slotted home to give the Swedes the lead.

Germany would go into half-time behind, but words to the effect of 'keep doing what you're doing,' would be Theune's instructions, according to defender Hingst.

Whatever was said, it worked, because Germany were level within a minute of the restart. Meinert, so influential throughout the tournament thanks to her partnership with Prinz, was able to level thanks to a finish from close range.

Germany were back in the game.

Neither team was able to find a winner within the remainder of the half, which meant the final would have to go into extra-time, with both teams having to prepare for the possibility of a Golden Goal being the difference.

Two minutes before the final whistle and an extra thirty minutes, however, coach Theune had sent on defender Nia Künzer to ensure her team did not concede while seeking out a winner.

That decision, much like her move to play the team's song in the stadium before the semi-final, would prove decisive.

Eight minutes into extra-time, Renate Lingor stood over a free-kick on the right side of the field, and swung a bending ball into the box. Künzer was there waiting to rise above everyone, and head past Caroline Jonsson in the Sweden goal.

Cue wild celebrations on the field and on the bench.

It was the most golden of Golden Goals. Germany had finally landed a World Cup at the fourth time of asking, and had claimed their first title outside of Europe.

Elation for the them, heartbreak for the second tournament running for Sweden.

Theune had built on the foundations laid by Gero Bisanz, and delivered an elusive World Cup.

Immediately after the triumph of the game, striker Prinz said in an interview for FIFA: 'It'll take ages for us to build another team as good as this one.'*

It wouldn't take that long, as this chapter explores later.

Despite such a heart-breaking loss for the Swedes, the two teams had developed a close relationship having played each other in so many big matches.

Nadine Angerer explains:

'I remember at the party after the final, someone from the German press said more than ten million people watched it on TV. More people in Germany watched the game than people who live in Sweden.

'We had developed a really good relationship with the Swedish players, so we partied with them after the final. The coaches had

* https://www.youtube.com/watch?v=HpuvTKaiZOY

agreed this beforehand, whoever won. But it was strange because the game had kicked off so early in the day, so some players went out or for a sleep before we partied later on.'

Women's football in Germany was finally on the map. As Angerer highlights, over ten million people watched the final on broadcaster ARD – but that was during normal time. That figure is reported to have increased to twelve million during extra-time. The match also fared well in Sweden too, with broadcaster TV4 attracting 3.8 million viewers during extra-time.*

Rainer Hennies, a freelance journalist who covered the Germany team in 2003, said the interest in the side was like something 'never seen before,' and outlined that Nia Künzer's goal was later voted Germany's Goal of the Year – male or female.

'Winning the match in Portland against the United States focused the media because Germany had not been in a World Cup Final for some time, so there were lots of journalists flying in to cover the final.

'Then there was the drama with Nia Künzer's Golden Goal header, which saw plenty of stories written.

'Back home the media hype was bigger than ever before. Women's football was suddenly the number one topic of the day.

'Back in Frankfurt at the "Römer", which is a big inner-city venue, thousands of people came to celebrate the team presenting itself with the cup on the Mayor's balcony. Nia Künzer's header in the final was later voted as the Goal of the Year on German TV (ARD).'

Germany had overcome their biggest hurdle, but with added interest in the team, the pressure now was how they would deal with being the team to beat, with more eyes inevitably on them.

---

* http://www.infrontsports.com/news/2003/10/broadcasters-strike-gold-in-2003-fifa-womens-world-cup-final/

Domestic football in Germany was also thriving. While crowd numbers didn't see a huge shift domestically, German teams were succeeding in Europe, with Turbine Potsdam and FFC Frankfurt winning the UEFA Women's Cup (now the Women's Champions League) in that period between 2003 and 2007. While domestic crowds were unaffected, the national team was seeing interest significantly increase.

'There was definitely more interest, we were suddenly getting thousands coming to watch the national team,' said Hingst.

'The game was starting to become more professional and you could see this in the Frauen-Bundesliga. I was at Turbine Potsdam and we had a run where we started to win more, but games were not on TV because there were still some big scores that you wouldn't want to see on television.'

Potsdam teammate Nadine Angerer agreed, saying that the increased professionalism of the game benefited both clubs and the national team.

'Potsdam's development was amazing. In 2001 we were not really professional. I remember we progressed every year and got better players. Young players stepped in, so we were successful. This helped the club get even more professional. In 2001 we didn't have a locker room, it was like a school, it was old East German locker rooms, some players even had to buy their own boots. When I left (in 2008) we had our own facility, locker rooms and washing machine. We had everything prepared.'

While clubs were becoming more professional, the national team would taste more success two years later when claiming yet another European title.

After a Bronze Medal at the 2004 Athens Olympics, the 2005 European Championships were held in the north-west of England, and having qualified easily, Germany were able to defend their title with some comfort.

They came through the group stages without conceding a goal, before defeating Finland 4-1 in the semi-final and Norway 3-1 in the final. Birgit Prinz, who now captained the side, scored in the final and finished joint second in the goal scoring charts alongside Conny Pohlers, with fellow forward Inka Grings topping the charts.

The 2005 triumph was the perfect way to end one of the longest associations with the team since its formation in 1982. It would be Tina Theune's last. She stepped down after the tournament.

Having been involved with the side for twenty-three years, she handed over the reins to her assistant, Silvia Neid, who would lead the country on the road to China to defend their World Cup title.

According to Hingst, the transition didn't have a huge impact on the team.

'Silvia had been assistant to Tina for much of her time as head coach, so things didn't change that much. Tina achieved a lot with the team, but we had a lot of good players that were used to winning, so the change in coach wasn't a problem.'

Germany's passage to China was a straightforward one, with eight wins from eight matches against Russia, Scotland, the Republic of Ireland and Switzerland. Inka Grings and Birgit Prinz continued to terrorise defences, while Kerstin Garefrekes continued to show her importance to the side.

One player growing frustrated with her lack of opportunities, however, was goalkeeper Angerer.

The German number two had played backup to Silke Rottenberg for ten years, and going into 2007 ahead of the World Cup, retirement was very much at the forefront of her mind.

'I was on the bench for ten years, then at the start of 2007 I finished my physiotherapy exams.

'The team went to play in a tournament in China at the start of that year, but I couldn't go because of my studies. I had decided at the start of that year that if I don't get selected for the World Cup, I am going to retire. I decided that I would be a physio and travel around the world if I don't play.

'I would have retired from football altogether. I loved my club, but it was all about Germany.'

Angerer was prepared to pack up the game she loved because warming the bench at international level just wasn't enough.

Then, an unfortunate episode for Rottenberg while the team was away in Asia, would change things completely.

'During my exams while the team was in China, I got a call and was told that Silke had torn her ACL.

'I had just accepted that I was probably going to retire, and then I get that call.'

Angerer was all of a sudden Germany's number one, and her focus now, along with that of the team, was on the World Cup draw, which took place at the Guanggu Science and Technology Exhibition Centre in Wuhan on Sunday, 22 April.

Germany were drawn alongside Japan, England and Argentina – three sides who had never been able to impose themselves at a World Cup.

The squad that Silvia Neid had picked had a very different look to that of 2003. There was no more Maren Meinert, Steffi Jones or Bettina Wiegmann, who had been replaced by the likes of Potsdam's forward Anja Mittag, Freiburg's midfielder Melanie Behringer, and Duisburg's defender Annike Krahn.

Nonetheless, Germany started the tournament on fire, thrashing Argentina 11-0 in Shanghai, with Prinz and Sandra Smisek both helping themselves to hat-tricks.

The next match was, as both Hingst and Angerer described, 'a wakeup call,' after a goalless draw with England, who were playing in their first World Cup since 1995. Neid's team had chances, but they just couldn't find a way through a stubborn England. Frustration for the Germans, but a precious point for England.

Any thoughts that the side had left their shooting boots in the dressing room after the Argentina match, were answered when Germany topped the group thanks to a 2-0 win over Japan – Prinz and Lingor on target for the reigning champions.

That set up a quarter-final in Wuhan against North Korea – a team that Angerer admits her side were not confident of beating.

'We watched their last group game in our hotel (a 2-1 defeat to Sweden). We didn't think we had a chance, they were machines, we felt there was no chance.'

That German pessimism that Angerer had spoken about during the 2003 World Cup, was evidently shared by the squad. As a result, they were instructed before the match to write down why they did not want to go home and why it was important that Germany remained in the tournament.

Hingst explains:

'We put up a big piece of paper and a pad, and everyone had to write why we cannot go back to Germany. I wrote that I wasn't ready to head back to my club in Sweden, while one player wrote, "I don't want to go back to university." Someone else said my vacation isn't booked for a few weeks. A lot of players wrote some funny stuff, so we brought that list to the game and it reminded us why we shouldn't go home. We also made a road to Shanghai with bullet points. First step was win first game, second was get out of the group, then qualify for the Olympics, then win our semi-final. It was step by step, game by game.'

It worked!

Germany ran out 3-0 winners against a team Hingst described as 'Duracell bunnies who run, and run, and run,' thanks to goals from Prinz, Lingor and young defender, Krahn.

That meant Norway in the semi-final in Tianjin, a side looking to reach their first final since 1995. Germany were too strong for their opponents, and went ahead when Norway's Trine Ronning turned in Prinz's cross into her own net after forty-three minutes.

Kerstin Stegemann's deflected effort doubled their lead on seventy-two minutes, before Martina Müller pounced on a mistake for the third goal just twelve minutes from time. While 3-0 made the game look comfortable, Angerer had to be in fine form to keep Norway out.

In the other semi-final, the United States were thumped by a Brazil side inspired by a twenty-one-year-old by the name of Marta.

A 4-0 win for the South Americans meant a first final, and a second consecutive semi-final defeat for the US, who would have been keen to avenge their 2003 defeat to the Germans.

There was added incentive for Germany to overcome their final opponents, with the team not being overly happy by wild celebrations from the Brazilians at their hotel following their semi-final win – a hotel that both teams had to share.

'Yes it's true, they won their semi-final and came in with their drums and music,' said Hingst.

'FIFA had the rule that the teams stayed in the same hotel and it annoyed us. Don't get me wrong, we know how to party, but it annoyed us because there was still the final to play – nobody had won yet.'

Angerer had watched that semi-final with a few of her teammates. After her apprehension on how her side would beat North Korea, the same questions would be asked when they watched Brazil dismantle the US.

'We watched it very closely,' she said.

'I remember Linda Bresonik saying, "I have never seen someone run so fast" when talking about North Korea. Then we watched the Brazil game with Martina Müller and a few others, and we were like, "How are we going to beat Brazil? How are we going to stop Marta? It's impossible."

'Silvia Neid was excellent, and she was honest. She said "Individually, we will struggle to stop them, but as a team, we can beat them." That gave us a lot of motivation because Silvia had a plan for everything; she even had a plan for Marta.'

That plan would need to be executed to perfection at the Hongkou Stadium, Shanghai, to stop a confident Brazil, who on their day were more than capable of beating anyone, which they proved in the semi-final against the US.

The opening minutes would give Angerer and her defence a good look at their opponents, with the likes of Marta and her fellow forward Cristiane, starting the match brightly.

'I remember the first three minutes against Brazil, it was such a fast game,' said Angerer.

'I remember staring at Marta, I adored her, and then remembered I needed to focus. I did my best to save her shots. Silvia said "don't look at Marta, just see the ball. It doesn't matter what tricks she does, don't react to her first movements, just see the ball." She kept repeating that, which I had to focus on.'

A goalless first half proved what a test Brazil were going to be for Germany and how closely matched the two sides were. But it was seven minutes after half-time that the deadlock was broken, and it came from the ever-reliable Prinz after she slotted home from inside the box after a square pass from Smisek. Germany had grabbed the advantage, but their resilience would be tested just twelve minutes after taking the lead – and Angerer would be the centre of attention.

Cristiane was played through with just the German keeper to beat, before Bresonik brought her down in the box, with the referee awarding Brazil a penalty.

A crowd of over thirty thousand fans, and nine million Germans watching at home, chewed their nails in anticipation. Marta would be taking the penalty, the top scorer in the tournament.

'My first reaction was that it was no penalty,' said Bresonik's fellow defender Hingst.

'Then my thought was "no worries." I knew Nadine was going to save it. She had had a great tournament and I just didn't see anyone beating her. I knew she was going to save it. When she saved it, the first reaction is to go crazy.'

Angerer was equal to Marta's effort, diving down to her right-hand side to thwart the classy Brazilian.

That save proved to be a huge moment in the match, as twenty-one-year-old Simone Laudehr met a corner four minutes from time to head Germany 2-0 in front, and put the game out of sight. Germany, all of a sudden, had breathing space, and a second World Cup was just minutes away.

Referee Tammy Ogston brought the game to a close shortly after, meaning Silvia Neid's team had become the first country to win back-to-back Women's World Cups, and they did it without conceding a single goal in the process.

In an interview with FIFA TV, Head Coach Neid described the achievement as 'sensational'.

'It was the perfect tournament, especially as we didn't even concede a goal.

'In the final, when Marta didn't convert the penalty, it was clear to me, that we'd win the final. They wouldn't score against us, and we'd finish the tournament without conceding. That's really something, not a single goal against us. That will never happen again – its sensational."*

Reuters reported that more than nine million people watched the final in Germany – 55 per cent of the market share, and much like 2003, thousands of people welcomed the team home as they paraded the World Cup for the second time.†

* https://www.youtube.com/watch?v=JCyVCNcC1qQ&t=557s
† https://uk.reuters.com/article/uk-soccer-women/womens-football-has-come-a-long-way-in-germany-idUKL1557188420071016

So what was key to the success of that team in winning back-to-back World Cups?

'Good coaches, smart players, positive characters, no egos – it's simple, but it's the key,' says Angerer.

'You need good coaches that challenge you, smart players that get what you want, and a good crew. As soon as you have egos it gets hard.'

German football would go from strength-to-strength, with clubs continuing to perform well in Europe, and the national team continuing to attract thousands to its matches. The team would make it a decade to remember two years later, by going on to win the European Championships in 2009 after thumping England 6-2 in the final in Finland.

A decade of dominance, which included back-to-back World Cups, meant Germany no longer 'had to hide behind the US,' says journalist Rainer Hennies. What they did, was make their mark on the global stage, and raise the bar even higher.

The footballing ability of the players that represented Germany during that era was clear for all to see, but it's leadership qualities that have seen a number of those players take up coaching roles within prominent clubs and the national team setup. Angerer has been instrumental in the development of goalkeepers at National Women's Soccer League (NWSL) club the Portland Thorns since taking up a coaching role at the end of December 2015, following her retirement. Hingst, meanwhile, has been part of the coaching setup at one of Europe's most dominant clubs, VfL Wolfsburg, since January 2016, and saw her club win a domestic double in 2018 after claiming the Frauen-Bundesliga (League) and DFB Pokal (German Cup).

Meanwhile, Steffi Jones, winner of the 2003 World Cup, replaced Neid as Head Coach of the national team in August 2016, but her tenure was short lived after a disappointing run of results saw her lose her job in March 2018. Fellow 2003 winner Martina Voss – now Martina Voss-Tecklenburg – replaced Jones in November 2018 after leaving her role as Switzerland Head Coach.

Maren Meinert, who formed such a lethal partnership with Birgit Prinz in 2003, is the Head Coach of Germany's Under-19s and 20s, with Silke Rottenberg her goalkeeper coach. In addition, Bettina Wiegmann works as her assistant and is also in charge of the Under-15s.

Women's football in Germany is in very good hands.

All the Glory

....

There's a tendency to narrow in on one, single, defining moment of a marquee sporting event. That one shot, pass or turnover – *that* is what changed the course of history, in our minds.

Those moments, however, while important, are typically the climax of a confluence of events. Which exact moments qualify also depends on our own inherent biases. The epic 1999 Women's World Cup final, for example, is a lot different from a Chinese perspective than it is from an American perspective.

Kristine Lilly's goal-line clearance in extra-time might be the big moment of the 1999 final, from China's perspective. US goalkeeper Briana Scurry had finally been beaten. In 1999, the Golden Goal rule still existed. That was to be the game-winner. That was China's moment to win the World Cup. But Lilly's forehead stood in the way, clearing the ball from danger and keeping the Americans alive. The US would soon thereafter prevail on penalty kicks.

Or, perhaps the moment the China players and fans remember is the one penalty kick which Scurry saved in the shootout. Scurry denied Liu Ying's tame effort on China's third spot-kick, the only attempt of the combined ten efforts not to be converted. Scurry took two huge steps forward – appearing to be about three yards off the line – to cut down the angle of the shot and eventually save it. Laws of the game state that she must stay on her line until the ball is kicked. No infraction was called, however, and the Americans grabbed control of the shootout.

That led to what Americans view as *the* defining moment of the 1999 Women's World Cup: Brandi Chastain steps up to take the fifth and decisive penalty kick for the United States. Wait. Brandi Chastain . . . and she's attempting it with her left foot? Yes. She swings through the ball, placing it high to her right. China goalkeeper Gao Hong dives the correct way, but the shot is perfectly placed. *Goal. Victory.* Chastain rips off her jersey to celebrate, clutching it as she drops to the ground in her black sports bra, teammates racing toward her in the distance. The large majority of the ninety thousand fans at Los Angeles' Rose Bowl are going nuts. This instant classic has its defining image, an enduring moment that would become larger than life. Ask someone about the 1999 World Cup, and Chastain is likely to be among the first topics raised.

To define the 1999 Women's World Cup by just one image, as is often done, is to overlook just how many things came together at once that magical summer. There were the important plays earlier in that match, and there were so many more things that had to happen to even make that moment under the blazing July sun possible. This entire tournament was redefining everything the world knew about women's soccer.

That the Americans were in the final after such a disastrous start to the knockout stage was a testament to their character and talent. That the Rose Bowl was sold out, and that the team attracted a travelling circus of fans and media, was a relief to players, who nearly never got the chance to have such a significant platform.

Chastain's penalty kick – and that final as a whole – will forever define the 1999 Women's World Cup. The process of even reaching that moment on 10 July 1999, provides the necessary context for just how remarkable the achievement was. That 1999 triumph was covered to the extreme in the public eye, the US players more than willing participants in the media storm which surrounded them. Among the extravagant occurrences – Chastain's penalty kick chief among them – were the overlooked moments which served as enablers of success for the 1999 event. Everything was intertwined.

FIFA awarded the United States the hosting rights to the 1999 Women's World Cup on 31 May 1996. The news was buried as a one-sentence bullet point among other agenda items. The awarding of 2002 men's World Cup hosting rights, to the joint bid from Japan and South Korea, was the headline news.

The US was a natural host for the 1999 women's event. The Americans had won the inaugural Women's World Cup in 1991 and finished third in 1995. Atlanta was hosting the 1996 Summer Olympics, the first Games which would feature women's soccer.

FIFA's initial plans for that 1999 Women's World Cup were modest. Officials proposed a scaled-down tournament held only on the East Coast and in small stadiums, no larger than fifteen thousand in capacity. They wanted to keep travel costs low and avoid potential embarrassment of empty stadiums on international television. The smashing attendance figures from the inaugural event in 1991 in China – which saw an average of over nineteen thousand fans per game and a crowd of sixty-three thousand for the final – were followed up by small crowds at the 1995 Women's World Cup in Sweden, where average attendance was just over four thousand fans per game, a number boosted by a crowd of seventeen thousand-plus for the final.*

American organisers, however, had a different idea. Two months after being awarded the hosting rights to the 1999 Women's World Cup, the inaugural women's soccer Olympic event kicked off. Over twenty-five thousand fans turned out at the Citrus Bowl in Orlando for the Americans' tournament-opening victory over Denmark; twenty-eight thousand showed up at the same venue two days later

* *The Girls of Summer*, Jere Longman (2000) p.30.

for a US victory over Sweden. Crowds were even larger in Miami for non-US games. The US women played a scoreless draw with China in front of over fifty-five thousand fans in Miami to round out group play, and then headed to Athens, Georgia, for the knockout round. They beat rivals Norway – who had embarrassed and infuriated them by their celebrations a year earlier in the World Cup semi-final – in front of over sixty-four thousand fans in the semi-finals, and they clinched the first gold medal in Olympic women's soccer in front of over seventy-six thousand fans.

Marla Messing, the president and CEO of the 1999 Women's World Cup, Alan I. Rothenberg, then the president of the US Soccer Federation, and Hank Steinbrecher, the federation's secretary general, took notice of the huge crowds. An idea was born: 1999 was going to be a major sporting event.

'In everything we did, we treated it as a major event,' Messing told Jere Longman in *The Girls of Summer*, a book documenting the team's 1999 tournament. 'Our choices in this country are stadiums with 5,000 or 10,000 seats, or stadiums with 50,000, 60,000, or 80,000 seats. Once you decide on 5,000 or 10,000 seats, the image of what you are selling is second class. Putting it in small stadiums would have sealed the fate of the tournament. You had to sell the image of a major event. Right away it was major because it's at Giants Stadium and the Rose Bowl.'*

Messing, who served as executive vice president of the successful USA 1994 men's World Cup, had her plan. FIFA, having seen the crowds at the 1996 Olympics and the success of 1994, was on board. Now came the difficult task of filling those huge American football stadiums for the biggest Women's World Cup yet, which was being expanded from twelve to sixteen teams. There were plenty of sceptics. Officials at the iconic RFK Stadium in Washington,

* *The Girls of Summer*, Jere Longman (2000) p.31.

D.C., scoffed at the Women's World Cup committee's offer of hosting group-stage games and a quarter-final, feeling they should have been awarded the final. They also weren't so sure the tournament would be a success.

'We were not confident that ... it would be profitable,' Mark McCullers, RFK's assistant stadium manager at the time, told the *Washington Post* in 1997.[*]

US players joined the grassroots marketing effort and by December 1998, two hundred thousand tickets had been sold.[†] That number was already nearly double the total attendance of the Sweden 1995 tournament, and confirmation that Messing and company were right to think big. But even they didn't realise just *how* big the tournament was going to be.

The opening match of the 1999 Women's World Cup was to be contested at Giants Stadium in East Rutherford, New Jersey, a rock's throw from New York City. The eight venues that the Women's World Cup committee selected would put the tournament in some of the largest media markets in the United States. Venue selection and scheduling was planned with the clear idea that the US women would start their campaign on the East Coast and, if all went as expected, bring their increasingly popular tour to California for the grand finale.

Significant traffic surrounded the US team bus as it approached Giants Stadium for that opening match. A sellout crowd of nearly seventy-nine thousand fans welcomed the US team to the country's largest metropolitan area, the players surrounded by towering

---

[*] https://www.washingtonpost.com/archive/sports/1997/11/19/rfk-balks-at-womens-world-cup-after-missing-out-on-final-game/72b38ec8-85af-4806-9636-d70c576eabb1/?noredirect=on&utm_term=.aabe4602f3b5
[†] *The Girls of Summer*, Jere Longman (2000) p.32.

stands of red, white and blue. Though players were publicly confident that fans would turn out for the match, the spectacle of the mid-June day at the iconic NFL stadium was a relief.

A nervy start for the Americans nearly put a damper on the atmosphere in the opening two minutes. Denmark's Gitte Krogh made a run behind the US defence and was in clear on net but pushed her right-footed shot just wide of the far post. Fittingly, Mia Hamm broke the deadlock in the seventeenth minute to settle the Americans. Hamm was the reluctant face of the team, a shy superstar thrust into the spotlight by growing media attention on these increasingly relatable players. It was Hamm's 110th career international goal, already a world record by that point.

Hamm's US career began in 1987 at the age of fifteen years, 140 days. She was still a teenager when she started for the US in their inaugural World Cup triumph in 1991. Over the course of the next decade, she would develop into the United States' top goal-scoring threat. Hamm had become a fan favourite by the start of 1999 – Mia t-shirts, Mia posters, Mia messages written in body paint. Boys and girls filled the stands for Mia, who achieved the one-name status which is synonymous with sporting legends. She was a role model and, for many, the introduction to the entire US team.

Nike got behind Hamm in earnest, boosting her profile to the wider public by featuring her in advertisements and naming a building after her at the company's Beaverton, Oregon, campus. Hamm's Gatorade commercial with basketball superstar Michael Jordan – which saw the two duel each other in several athletic competitions, set to the song, 'Anything you can do, I can do better' – boosted her profile further.

American media took notice. Win or lose, goal or no goal, Hamm was the player that journalists wanted to speak with. Long a reserved personality, Hamm used the opportunities – as best she could – to speak about her teammates.

'I'm not a real extrovert,' she told reporters at the time, one of the greater understatements. 'And as a kid I was usually in the background. So, it was easier for me to communicate with people through sports and get to know them that way. Sports were a way for me to fit in.'*

Hamm scored just twice in that 1999 World Cup; no US player scored more than three goals. The Americans were shut out of the individual awards for best player and top goal-scorer, a testament to their team approach more than an indictment of any individual player. They leaned on each other.

Julie Foudy and Kristine Lilly scored in the second half of that opening match against Denmark to lift the US to a 3-0 victory. A 7-1 whooping of Nigeria followed at Soldier Field in Chicago in front of over sixty-five thousand fans before the US flew to Boston for their final group match. US players were welcomed to Logan Airport by a marching band as they were showered with flowers. Americans were catching World Cup fever. A 3-0 victory over a tricky North Korea team in front of fifty thousand-plus fans at Foxboro Stadium sealed first place in the group for the United States. Germany awaited in the quarter-finals.

Everyone remembers the 1999 final against China. It was the type of 'Where were you?' moment which would inspire an entire generation of young players and prove that women's sports could be major events. Often overlooked in the United States' run to the 1999 title, however, is that quarter-final against Germany.

Chastain was the starting left fullback for the United States. She played sparingly as a forward during the team's 1991 World Cup triumph under Anson Dorrance, and Tony DiCicco dropped her

* https://www.socceramerica.com/publications/article/8821/us-women-quotes-from-mia-hamm-teleconference.html

from the 1995 World Cup team. Hungry to return to the team after its heartbreak at that tournament, Chastain reinvented herself as a defender and assumed the starting role on the left side for the 1996 Olympics. By 1999, any hint of that conversion being experimental was gone. Here stood Brandi Chastain, defender.

Her big moment in Pasadena nearly never came to pass, however. Early-game jitters were becoming a concerning trend for the Americans at the 1999 World Cup. Denmark hadn't capitalised in the opener, but the 7-1 rout of Nigeria began with a goal for the underdogs less than two minutes into the match, a product of a poor clearance. Scurry had to be quick off her line two minutes into the quarter-final to prevent a clear opportunity for Germany.

Five minutes in, disaster struck. German star Maren Meinert played a hopeful ball in behind the United States' defence. Chastain was comfortably the first to arrive to deal with the situation, and, facing her own goal, she decided to play the ball back to Scurry, who could clear it forward. Chastain didn't look up, however. Scurry was aggressively coming off her line to claim the ball with her hands and, not ready for the back pass, could only watch Chastain's pass trickle past her and into the net. *Own goal. Germany leads.*

Chastain's look of disbelief said it all. US players knew the weight of the moment and Chastain knew that the task just became more difficult. But Carla Overbeck, the team's captain, knew that there were still eighty-five minutes of soccer to be played. She found Chastain and delivered a simple message: 'We need you.'

Eleven minutes later, the US was level. Tiffeny Milbrett pounced on a loose ball that the Germans failed to deal with, and calmly slotted the ball into the lower corner from 12 yards away for her third goal of the tournament. The US had a temporary advantage at the time; Bettina Wiegmann had gone off the field for several minutes to get medical treatment after taking an elbow to the face in midfield.

Wiegmann returned to the field shortly after Milbrett's goal and, in stoppage time of the first half, delivered a near-crushing blow to the Americans. The match looked like it would head into half-time level at 1-1, but Wiegmann found space 20 yards from the United States' goal and unleashed a left-footed shot into the side netting. Germany led 2-1 and took all the momentum into half-time. The American dream of winning a Women's World Cup on home soil was forty-five minutes from ending.

Fourteen years later, the late DiCicco would recall in an ESPN documentary that his message to the team at half-time was very simple: 'The only thing I really remember saying is, "Don't let your dream end today. We can play better. We have to play better." '*

They did just that. Chastain had her redemption four minutes after half-time. Hamm served the ball deep to the back post on a US corner kick and it got redirected back across the face of the goal, six yards out. Chastain was there to swing her right boot through it and put it into the side netting for the US equaliser. Her relief was palpable: mouth agape, she ran a short distance as she looked to the sky before dropping onto her back with her arms spread wide to form a 'T', only soon to grab her forehead in a sign of disbelief. Her goal, this time in the correct net, had the US back in a match she thought she might have cost them.

Tides had turned, and the Americans began knocking on the door for the go-ahead goal. Chastain found space on another header before Hamm nearly got in behind on a solo counterattack. Hamm found space again in the sixty-fifth minute, but her half-chance was deflected out for a US corner kick. Shannon MacMillan, the team's super sub, entered the match and went straight to the corner. Her first touch of the ball was an assist on the winning goal – a driven

* (not the original video): https://www.youtube.com/watch?v=1EKou -qmnjc

cross, head height, to the near post, where Joy Fawcett redirected the ball into the net. USA 3, Germany 2.

The Americans clamped down defensively and saw out the victory. Crisis had been averted. The team would be congratulated – for the first of two times at this tournament – in the locker room after the match by President Bill Clinton.

They were headed west, to Palo Alto, California, for a semi-final against Brazil at Stanford Stadium on 4 July – Independence Day. Opening-minute nerves were put to rest in that match. Cindy Parlow opened the scoring just five minutes in, pouncing on a mistake from the Brazilian goalkeeper, and Michelle Akers added an insurance goal from the penalty spot ten minutes from time. Scurry came up huge in the match, denying the Brazilians with several spectacular saves to preserve the clean sheet.

The Road to Pasadena, as the US women's national team's nine-game preparation tour was called in 1999, was headed to its final destination. China awaited on 10 July.

A full week between the semi-finals and the final was ample time to hype the biggest sporting event of the year – and the timing of the tournament on the wider US sports calendar was perfect to maximise attention. Mid-July is traditionally the slowest time of the year for sports in the US; the day after the Major League Baseball All-Star Game is referred to within the industry as the slowest day in sports. Even baseball, with its tireless daily schedule, takes that one day off. Hockey and basketball seasons are finished, and preseason hasn't yet begun for professional or college football.

Over five hundred reporters covered the 1999 Women's World Cup final.* The 'circus', as DiCicco would call it, was an everyday thing the team had to deal with. The pressure was immense. The

* *The Girls of Summer*, Jere Longman (2000) p.30.

US team attracted thousands of fans and hordes of media just for their practice sessions. Players were peppered with questions and inundated with autograph requests. They were bona fide rock stars; they were America's team. Filtering out the distractions was easier said than done.

Yet US players stayed grounded and adapted. Those who had been around for the largely anonymous World Cup triumph of 1991 were witnessing the incredible progress of the sport right in front of them. The 'soccer evangelists' role that former Head Coach Anson Dorrance had spoken of was paying off on home soil.

'We always understood the big picture,' Foudy said. 'It wasn't just, "oh we're competing for a World Cup." We have a chance to set an example and set a standard. We realised, too, that there wasn't a lot of examples or standards on the women's side. It was our opportunity and our privilege to be able to do that. It came with a lot of pressure, but it also came with this great sense of purpose. People say, "Were you surprised by the turnout and the reaction?" And I say no, because that is what we had dreamt of and envisioned. That's what we had told US Soccer would happen. If they had marketed it, people would come. It will be a big deal; you have to make it a big deal.'

In many ways, players dealt with newfound fame simply by being themselves. Foudy was among the chief pranksters on the squad – and she also happened to be the unofficial team videographer. She and her teammates still share endless stories about the fun they had during their long spells of time together, from months-long training camps to life on the road during the tournament. Silliness kept them grounded – and it kept them sane.

Among the illuminating windows into their personalities was the scene at their hotel the night before that pressure-packed opening match of the World Cup. Chastain had posed nude for *Gear* magazine, covering herself only with a soccer ball. Her teammates couldn't pass up the opportunity for friendly banter. 'If you're going to pose naked, you're going to hear it from the team,' Foudy said.

So US players recorded a satire video – players covered their otherwise exposed bodies comedically with everything from crossword puzzles to shin guards. A team meeting was called, supposedly to watch a news feature that a national station produced on the team . . . except the tape in the VCR was their video poking fun at Chastain. The whole staff was in on the joke, coaches and all – everyone except Chastain, that is.

That DiCicco allowed for the silliness, at a time when plenty of coaches would crack down and demand concentration, was part of his superior management. DiCicco knew that all his players were adults and that they knew their limits. He knew that they wouldn't get carried away and lose focus.

'He celebrated that rather than try to tamper it down, which is the brilliance of his method and his coaching style,' Foudy said. 'Because he let us be, but also he was strong enough to say, "bring it in." And he knew also there would be a lot of pressure with that tournament, and this helps to have fun and diffuse that pressure in different ways. He was just a great players' manager in that sense.'

DiCicco, as the legend goes, would walk on the field each day – practice or game – and scream, 'I love my job!' He was coaching the best women's soccer team in the world and he was getting paid to do so. The coach was a reflection of his players. A humility within the group made players relatable to the average person and was a huge reason for the team's rise in popularity. They had captured the attention of a nation thirsty for a positive story – heroes to cheer for – and they were now one victory away from cementing their legacy.

Such a huge spotlight on the team stood in stark contrast with the 1991 US team's march to the World Cup title, which was more or less done in secret, half a world away in China. The talent on that '91 squad is considered by many to be on par with the '99ers – the first generation of players just never had the platform to earn the plaudits.

Michelle Akers owned that inaugural Women's World Cup, scoring ten goals as one-third of the United States' 'Triple-Edged Sword' front line. Eight years later, Akers was thirty-three years old and playing in a much deeper midfield role for the United States as she battled through the Chronic Fatigue and Immune Dysfunction Syndrome under the hot summer sun. She had managed the condition for years, and her move to midfield was meant to mitigate the wear and tear put on her body.

Still, daily fluctuations in energy levels were her reality. Her mornings would begin with a cup of coffee and a mental check before anything else. *How am I feeling today?* The question wasn't the type of pick-me-up motivation it might be for the average person. For Akers, it was about assessing how difficult the day ahead might be. Energy levels fluctuated between days and within matches.*

'The only way I can describe the sensation,' she wrote, in her 2000 autobiography, about the in-game walls she would hit, 'is to say it's like trying to play in a dark tunnel. Awareness of my surroundings fades along with my peripheral vision. All I can see or focus on is whatever is right in front of me – if I can just manage to really, really concentrate.'†

If Akers didn't openly discuss her chronic fatigue, it would otherwise be difficult to believe that she, the 5-foot-10 wrecking ball and heart of the US team, struggled as much as she did. Her skill was undeniable. Akers scored five goals in one game at the 1991 World Cup, a record which still stands. She continued to dominate in her move to the midfield, despite playing a much different role. Her

* *The Game and the Glory*, Akers (2000) p. 22.
† *The Game and the Glory*, Akers (2000) p. 37.

performances at the 1999 World Cup, which capped off over a decade of dominance in a United States jersey, finally gave her the spotlight she deserved. Akers and Chinese star Sun Wen would in 2000 be jointly named FIFA's women's players of the century.

Media gravitated toward Hamm. Chastain's penalty kick and celebration made for the iconic image of the '99ers. But Akers was the team's heart and soul. She left her body on the field, enduring the debilitating fatigue and migraines – among other symptoms – which temporarily knocked her down. She fought through eight career knee operations. She avoided dairy, bread and alcohol; hydration was an involved task which often included intravenous. She kept a container of coffee close by for energy boosts pregame and at half-time.

'Out of all people to get chronic fatigue, it's an irony because it's a player who is the hardest workhorse of all of us,' Foudy said. 'Her work was all that she did. She went out early and she shot. Her being the best finisher in the world and one of the best scorers in the world wasn't a coincidence. She grinded it out. She was a grinder. That was the example I saw every day. When you got to practice, she was already out there with a bag of balls.'

By 10 July 1999, that grind had one more game of consequence left in it. Akers had laid out her body throughout the tournament, as she always does, and she had reinjured her shoulder at practice the day before the final. This World Cup final, against a strong, skilled and physical China team, was going to require a monumental effort. Through forty-five minutes, with the game scoreless, it nearly took everything Akers had.

'By the time we got to the locker room, I was so exhausted and sick I felt as if I were going to die,' she later wrote.*

Nobody not named Michelle Akers could quite comprehend what she was feeling that day, having already started four of the

* *The Game and the Glory*, Akers (2000) p. 34.

Americans' five games over the course of three weeks. DiCicco gave her the entire game off against North Korea to round out group play, which appeared to help re-energise her, but every day was a new challenge. This China game was proving particularly trying.

Just seconds of stoppage time remained in the second half when China earned a corner kick. Liu Ying struck a driven ball toward the near post, right in that sweet spot between the goalkeeper and six-yard-box which always wreaks havoc on defences – and much like the winning goal the US scored in that quarter-final comeback against Germany. Scurry came off her line to punch the ball away. Akers zeroed in on the ball, seeing nothing but its flight as she went to clear it away.

The ball bounced up and the Americans cleared it. Akers laid flat on the ground, face down, and slowly rose up, holding her head as the full-time whistle blew. The two teams were headed to extra-time. Akers, however, was headed to the bench. She had been sandwiched between her own goalkeeper and an opposing player. Akers had picked herself up countless times, but this one was different. She was replaced by Sara Wahlen as overtime began. Television cameras flashed to Akers on the sideline as she sat on the US bench, slumped over with cold, soaked, white towels draped over her head to cool her off and shield her from the brutal summer sun hitting the exposed field at the Rose Bowl.

Akers was soon taken to the locker room, where she would later detail the haziness that she experienced as she navigated not a concussion, by doctors' diagnoses, but complete exhaustion. She would require four litres of IV solution to stabilise and rehydrate her body, her jersey cut off her to more immediately administer the liquid. Her teammates would need to win this match with their heartbeat underneath the concrete stands, Akers just barely aware of what was going on.

As far as the game was concerned, the US just lost its most dominant presence in the middle of the park. China, whose strong offence had been bottled up for the first ninety minutes, saw an opportunity.

Golden Goal was in effect in FIFA competitions once again, meaning the two, fifteen-minute extra-time periods made for a sudden-death affair. China began attacking through the middle, in the absence of that imposing number ten jersey standing in their way. Sun Wen charged into that space in the first half of extra-time and fired a left-footed shot which deflected out of bounds. Another China corner kick.

Kristine Lilly quickly poured water over her head from a bottle kept next to Scurry's goal. She capped the bottle and immediately grabbed the goal post with her left hand. This was her post to guard, just in case Scurry got beat.

Liu Ying served the ball up again, this time to the back post. Fan Yunjie rose above a pair of Americans to win the header, sending it back across goal. Scurry was beat. But Lilly – all 5 feet, 4 inches of her – was standing on the line. She hopped and headed the ball back into play with her forehead. That clearance is as important a play as any in US soccer history. Lilly, like so many of her teammates, was an unsung hero, a relative term that was the product of a holistic team approach.

The match remained scoreless through extra-time and moved to penalty kicks, where Scurry made that controversial save and Chastain converted that winning penalty kick and produced that iconic celebration. Even within those penalty kicks there occurred layers of events which all needed to come together for the Americans.

Hamm initially didn't want to be one of the five shooters, but US assistant coach Lauren Gregg, who had meticulously tracked penalty kicks in practice and planned for this scenario, told Hamm that she was the team's goal-scorer, and her team needed her. Hamm agreed; no more convincing needed.

Gregg still needed to have another conversation. DiCicco wanted Chastain to be the fifth kick-taker, and he wanted her to take the kick with her left foot to give China goalkeeper Gao Hong a different look. Chastain was mildly surprised but took the instructions in her stride.

Xie Huilin converted the first penalty kick for China, and Overbeck answered for the US. The teams traded successful kicks again before Scurry's save on Liu Ying's attempt, and then each team once again successfully converted. Sun Wen kept China alive by converting their fifth and final kick. The US needed to score. Up stepped Chastain to power the ball high and to her right, into the goal and past Gao Hong.

The crowd of over ninety thousand at the Rose Bowl was ecstatic, along with some eighteen million Americans watching on television, a soccer record which would stand until the United States' 2015 Women's World Cup triumph. President Clinton would once again be on hand to congratulate the team in person, calling the match the most exciting sporting event he'd seen.

The unprecedented attention on that 1999 final inspired a generation of female athletes, served as the catalyst for the first attempt at a US pro league – the Women's United Soccer Association – and set the standard for women's sport. It showed that treating women's sports as just that – sports – could be done in a big way. Many players on the 2015 World Cup-winning squad were inspired by that 1999 team; some were even in the stands that day. But growth of the sport since has hardly been linear.

'I think the disappointing thing is that I don't think it has had [a big enough effect] – or maybe it has taken too long for the effect to be fully felt,' says Foudy, reflecting on the legacy of 1999. 'We thought it would inspire other sports to hold big events and to do it in a meaningful way, and a big way. It's just too slow. We thought other countries would start funding their women's programmes

– you can see how long that has taken. That's where I get frustrated. I think it could have and should have had a much bigger effect in the women's sporting landscape.'

WUSA would last only three seasons, folding on the eve of the 2003 Women's World Cup, which was relocated to the United States at short notice after the SARS outbreak in China. Crowd sizes were more modest this time, and the Americans finished third, just as they would in 2007. Nearly a decade later, the fire of '99 felt like it had reduced to a flicker in the US as a new pro league finally got off the ground, six years after the first attempt failed. The US women's national team could no longer fill the Rose Bowl. Even after winning the 2008 Olympic gold medal, the Americans returned home for a victory tour which drew weak crowds. Less than five thousand people showed up at a cavernous Giants Stadium which nine years earlier sold out to commence the Americans' World Cup campaign. The 1999 World Cup was an unmitigated success but, once again, the sport was desperately in need of a jolt.

One Day in Dresden

....

The 2011 World Cup is when the United States women became rock stars. Their triumph four years later cemented their status as the world's most high-profile women's sports team, but 2011 was the year those roots truly began to take hold.

New York City gave a hero's welcome to the twenty-three players and their staff when they returned from Germany in mid-July 2011. The Americans had just captured the attention of the nation with the most epic of comebacks in the quarter-finals and went on to appear in their first World Cup final since that magical 1999 triumph on home soil.

Upon returning home in 2011, players did all the standard New York media rounds that come with the fanfare of American athletic greatness: late-night and early-morning talk shows, daytime news interviews, promotional events and, of course, autographs for the hordes of screaming fans.

Such festivities were not entirely new to the American women. They were, at the time, the two-time defending Olympic gold-medallists, and they would make it three in a row the following year in London. Players had been on these publicity tours before. And this was how they envisioned returning from Germany that summer: as champions – as heroes. Swathes of fans worshipped them as they parted seas of human bodies simply to walk from a bus into the entrance of a television studio or their hotel. Players were lauded for their efforts and showered with congratulations. *Champions*, some of the general populous thought.

How awkward, the players thought, in reply. It took reminding for some that the US women did not win the 2011 World Cup. They finished runners-up, falling to Japan in the final, playing antagonists to the most incredible and unlikely of Women's World Cup stories to date. Japan – a team that had never previously even been to a semi-final, and a country reeling from a catastrophic earthquake and subsequent tsunami just a few months earlier – had won the World Cup.

'I think because of the Brazil game – the quarter-final – that people thought we won the World Cup, because that one game kind of encompassed and defined the World Cup for us,' US forward Abby Wambach explained.

Wambach was the centrepiece of attention. She was the hero who scored *that* goal which made front-page headlines and dominated sports television shows just over a week earlier. Her header in that quarter-final against Brazil tied the game in the 122nd minute – at the time, the latest goal ever scored in an official FIFA competition. It was quintessential American grit, the never-say-die, red-white-and-blue flag-waving, undying belief that US players have long taken pride in.

Their emotional roller coaster in Germany temporarily sheltered them from the pandemonium back home. Upon returning to the US, however, the players quickly gained a sense of how much attention their run to the final had attracted.

'The moment that I realised that things were going to be different from there on was actually when we returned, after having lost to Japan in the final, and we were on a bus from the airport,' Wambach said. 'We had just gotten off the plane from Germany and we still had to go and do the New York media tour. Even though we lost, all the TV stations, they wanted us on.

'It was the moment that we were pulling into our hotel room that there was just a mob of a crowd. It was like, "What the heck is going on? What is happening here? Why are we staying at this hotel that is crazy outside?" And as we got closer, as the bus stopped, I saw that they were all wearing USA jerseys. I looked at Christie Rampone sitting next to me and I said, "Holy shit, they are here for us. We didn't even win the World Cup." '

Even in the disappointment of defeat, US players recognised that this was a special moment. One incredible week in Germany created what would become a much more sustained ripple effect in the United States for women's soccer. There had been optimism before – no more so than following the wildly successful 1999 Women's World Cup on home soil – but this time felt different. The climate around the sport and the country was changing. Players were still heartbroken from the loss to Japan, but they did their best to embrace an onslaught of positive attention.

'When you get back from losing and you are still being revered as champions . . . it was a little bit weird for us,' Wambach said. 'Even though we lost, we defied the odds in that game against Brazil, and it felt like it was a way for Americans to define who we are. We never quit, we play until the last minute. Even against the odds, there are still miracles that happen, and I think we kind of personified that feeling that Americans were needing to have.'

The difference was jarring between their welcome home and their send-off. This was a team that suddenly everyone knew. Nobody could have predicted that just one month earlier.

It's 5 June 2011 in Harrison, New Jersey – a short skip over the Hudson River from New York – and the US women are playing their World Cup send-off game against Mexico at Red Bull Arena. This is the last match the Americans will play before boarding a plane to Germany in search of a World Cup title that has eluded the prestigious programme since 1999. The New York metro area provides both media opportunities to spread the word and easy travel to Europe after the match. At least one of those things was true.

An announced crowd of 5,852 is on hand at the twenty-five thousand-seat Red Bull Arena for one final look at this US team before the World Cup. The stadium is a sea of blue plastic seats. Sunil Gulati, then president of the US Soccer Federation, would spend part of his half-time media availability defending the poor attendance, noting that a Sunday afternoon in the late spring, when so many youth soccer players and their parents are off participating in games of their own, is always a difficult sales proposition.

One day earlier, a few hours up Interstate-95, in Foxborough, Massachusetts, the US men's national team attracted a crowd of over sixty thousand fans as they got whooped, 4-0, by reigning world champions Spain. The buzz which surrounded the US women's team over a decade earlier had faded, the legends of that generation now retired.

'If you're talking about recreating the magic moment of '99, no, that's not going to happen,' Gulati told reporters. 'We're not at home. It won't be that iconic. Very few things can compete with that in any sport. And the history of women's leagues is that they're a struggle.'

'If you're talking about winning the World Cup, that's very possible,' Gulati said. 'This team has a record unmatched by anyone around the world.'*

Gulati was defensive and the US players were more hopeful than anything. They intertwined their success playing as the national team to the overall future of their sport and their livelihood. Bringing home trophies was not just about winning; it was about surviving. Winning another World Cup was, ostensibly, the way to keep their league alive.

* https://www.nydailynews.com/sports/more-sports/tiny-red-bull-arena-crowd-represents-hurdle-u-s-women-soccer-faces-entering-world-cup-germany-article-1.126002

Women's Professional Soccer (WPS) was in the middle of its third season when the 2011 World Cup rolled around. Three teams had already folded, another moved down to an amateur division, and the iconic Washington Freedom brand had been cheaply renamed after an internet phone product and relocated to Boca Raton, Florida. All indications were that this second attempt at a professional women's soccer league in the US would end after three seasons, just as the previous incarnation had. The Women's United Soccer Association kicked off in 2001 in an attempt to capitalise on the attention the US team captured at the 1999 Women's World Cup. But the WUSA shut down after the 2003 season – an announcement that came just a few days before the start of the 2003 Women's World Cup, which was back in the United States after the SARS outbreak in China forced a relocation of the tournament.

A meagre crowd in New Jersey for the Americans' final game before the 2011 World Cup didn't inspire confidence in the sport's overall health. The weird match that day was fitting for the overall temperature of the women's game at the time. The Americans outshot Mexico 34-4, dominating but failing to score until the second minute of added time in the second half. This was the Mexico team which eight months earlier defeated the US in World Cup qualifying, producing the most shocking upset in the sport's history. That result forced the Americans – ranked first in the world – to win a two-leg playoff against Italy in order even to qualify for the World Cup. The result was unthinkable heading into the tournament: Mexico had never defeated the US, and the Americans had won every single World Cup qualifying match that they ever played. A team once viewed as invincible suddenly had an air of uncertainty around it. Now, the World Cup was here, and the US women were in a precarious place.

*   *   *

Dresden served as the site of the Americans' opening game of the 2011 World Cup. The opposition, North Korea, was both familiar and formidable. This was the fourth consecutive Women's World Cup in which the two teams were slated to meet in the group stage of the tournament, and the encounters had become increasingly tight. The US won the first two clashes handily, but the two teams drew, 2-2, at the 2007 World Cup in China. North Korea entered this 2011 World Cup ranked as the eighth-best team in the world.

In addition to North Korea, Group C featured Sweden, ranked fifth in the world. Only two of the four teams – Colombia rounded out the group – would advance to the knockout stage. One of the world's top-ten teams would be bowing out early.

North Korea had long been an enigma as a team difficult to scout. Defensive discipline and tactical sophistication were staples of the team, no matter which coach was in charge or which players were selected. A scoreless first half between the two sides only confirmed as much, but the US got on the board nine minutes after half-time thanks to a beautifully placed, headed goal from Lauren Cheney, who, at the time, was a somewhat surprising starter in place of Megan Rapinoe. Defender Rachel Buehler added an insurance goal for the Americans in the seventy-sixth minute, and the 2-0 victory got them off to the start they needed.

What followed for North Korea was a loss to Sweden and a scoreless draw with Colombia, an otherwise forgettable World Cup. Away from the field, however, the team's tournament was downright bizarre: five North Korean players failed drug tests. The first two tested positive following the team's second group match and they were suspended for the final group game. Upon that news, FIFA decided to drug test the entire team, and three more players failed.

North Korean officials presented their excuse to FIFA: players had accidentally taken steroids with traditional Chinese medicines based on musk deer glands . . . to treat players who had been struck by lightning during training camp prior to the World Cup. North Korean officials first mentioned the lightning strike after losing their opening match to the US, but they refused to elaborate. FIFA, along with most of the rest of the world, wasn't buying it. This was the biggest doping scandal at a major international tournament since Diego Maradona's ban in the 1994 men's World Cup, and the fallout was immense: North Korea was fined $400,000 USD and banned from the next Women's World Cup in 2015.[*]

The US, meanwhile, moved forward. Colombia made their Women's World Cup debut in 2011 and entered the tournament with zero expectations from the outside world. The US was expected to comfortably handle the debutantes, and they did just that. Heather O'Reilly pounced on a poor giveaway by Colombia twelve minutes into the match and fired a knuckling shot into the upper corner to score what was to be one of the goals of the tournament. The eleven American players on the field celebrated the goal with a military-style salute, a nod to the local US military community, some of whom attended the match.[†]

Rapinoe scored a second goal five minutes after half-time and added to the festive atmosphere, grabbing a field microphone and celebrating by singing, 'Born in the USA'. Carli Lloyd added another goal seven minutes later and the US cruised to a 3-0 victory.

And then came Sweden. Both the Americans and the Swedes had already guaranteed advancement by the time they met in

* https://www.nydailynews.com/sports/more-sports/north-korea-play-ers-flunk-steroid-test-women-world-cup-germany-article-1.161003 & http://www.espn.com/espnw/news-commentary/2015worldcup/article /12912763/strange-story-north-korea-soccer
† https://www.stripes.com/sports/u-s-women-s-soccer-team-scores-high-with-military-fans-1.147937 & https://www.ussoccer.com/stories/ 2014/03/17/13/32/2011-best-of-awards

Wolfsburg on 6 July, each team having won its first two matches of the tournament. The group-stage meeting was a tradition for these two rivals: this was the third straight World Cup in which they had been drawn in the same group, a tradition which carried on in 2015 and 2019.

The winner of this match would top the group, while the loser would face the first-place team from Group D. Wambach's second-half goal was not enough to erase a pair of Swedish strikes in the first half, leaving the Swedes as 2-1 victors and handing the Americans their first-ever loss in the group stage of a World Cup.

Of more importance were the ramifications for the rest of the tournament. Sweden would now play the second-place team from Group D: the young, upstart Australians. The US would now face a difficult quarter-final opponent in old rival Brazil, back in Dresden.

Just over a minute has ticked off the clock, and it's difficult to imagine a better start for the United States. Midfielder Shannon Boxx serves a low cross in the direction of Wambach, and Brazilian defender Daiane slices her clearance into her own goal. *One-nil, USA.*

This is the type of start that teams dream of for a knockout-round match. But just over an hour later, everything changes. Marta, Brazil's once-in-a-lifetime legend, has used her impressive agility to squeeze between US defenders Christie Rampone and Rachel Buehler while chasing down a bouncing ball in the United States' penalty box. With the deft flick of her left foot, Marta seamlessly loops the ball over the heads of both defenders and towards the goal, all while keeping her stride to ensure she gets back to the ball first.

Buehler, having allowed Marta to get goal-side of her, now has a decision to make: let her go, and likely allow her to score Brazil's equalising goal, or foul her. Buehler – nicknamed, 'the Buehldozer,' for her physical play – opts for the foul, pulling down Marta by her canary yellow shirt as the Brazilian tries to shoot.

Whistle. Foul. Red Card.

The Americans are reduced to ten players and will have to play the final twenty-plus minutes of regulation at a disadvantage. Brazil also has a penalty kick, one which is likely to tie the match. In goal for the US stands Hope Solo, the legendary goalkeeper whose speciality is the spectacular – including saving penalty kicks. Longtime Brazilian forward Cristiane stares her down, lining up the shot with her left foot.

Goalkeepers largely have two options on penalty kicks: guess and risk diving completely the wrong way or wait to try to track the ball and hope to react in time to a shot taken from just 12 yards away. It's easy to see why many prefer to guess: there often isn't enough time to react to a shot from that close. Goalkeeping has evolved through the years, though, and the guessing game is not blind luck, but a combination of scouting reports, intuition and reading body language.

Here, Cristiane appears to be forecasting her shot – or, perhaps, that's what she wants Solo to think. Cristiane's run-up is short – just two steps. Logically, she'll want to slot the ball to her left; pushing it across her body, to her right, is a much more difficult task with a short run-up to generate power. And indeed, the penalty is relatively poor, hit tamely and at hip-height. Solo tracks it the entire way, diving to her left (Cristiane's right) and swatting the ball away. The Americans have dodged danger and might just get out of this game despite their disadvantage.

Only, referee Jacqui Melksham blows the play dead as the Americans celebrate. Melksham is pointing back to the spot for a re-take, to the dismay of Solo and her teammates. Solo is cautioned for protesting and confusion hangs over the near-capacity crowd. Television replays depicting the referee's view show the slightest of infractions by Rampone. The American captain stepped into the penalty area a fraction of a second prior to Cristiane's kick. That is against the rules, but the marginal nature of this particular infraction means it is rarely called. Rampone has one foot in the box as the ball leaves Cristiane's foot.

So there sits the ball, again placed on the white spot centred 12 yards from goal. Players from each team are once again standing on the outskirts of the penalty area. Solo is once again standing on her line, crouched over as she intensely stares at a yellow jersey threatening to unravel her World Cup dream. The face staring back at her is different this time, however.

Marta, the player who earned the penalty, is standing over the ball. She, too, lines up a left-footed shot, but she will give herself a longer run-up than her teammate did. Marta also decides to shoot across her body, to her right, placing the ball lower than Cristiane did. This time, Solo guesses and moves in the opposite direction.

Goal, Brazil.

Now the Americans are flirting with trouble. They've long been known for their resilience, their ability to win games when logic and probability say they shouldn't. It's why they won two of the first three Women's World Cups. It's why they entered this World Cup as two-time defending Olympic gold-medallists. And it's why there isn't full-on panic amid the chaos. They are still in this game – it's only 1-1, after all – but the warm July sun is wearing on a team playing with one less player than the opponents. The clock ticks off until ninety, and the game heads to thirty minutes of extra-time.

There's an accomplishment in just getting to that ninety-minute mark when down a player. *One chance; all you need in extra-time is one chance.* That's the message that Wambach tells her team.

But that one chance comes for Brazil less than two minutes into extra-time. US defenders collectively get pulled out of position toward the sideline while their help defenders get caught ball-watching. Marta is standing in the centre of the box, a few feet from the penalty spot, watching the play develop. The ball is crossed and

Marta switches from standing to sprinting. She extends her left leg and swings it like a pendulum, softly looping the ball over the heads of her and her trailing defender and toward the far post. The angle and the approach seem nearly impossible. Solo chases the ball across the goal line, tracking it from her near-post to her far-post.

Marta turns and watches hopefully as the ball travels across the face of the goal and toward the far post, time having seemingly slowed down. She half-skips with her left arm partially lifted, mouth open – the look of a player willing the ball into the net, ready to celebrate what could be a monumental moment for her and her country. The ball kisses the inside of the metal post and bounces into the net. Brazil leads.

Marta celebrates as if she knows she just won the match. She's well aware of the weight of the moment. She is the most talented player women's soccer has ever seen, but Brazil has long underachieved, having never won a World Cup or Olympic gold medal on the women's side. Much of that is blamed on the federation's lack of investment in its women's team, and the players – Marta more than any other – carry that burden into each major tournament.

Four years earlier, Brazil came as close as ever, at the expense of the US. On that September day in 2007, Marta and her teammates embarrassed the US, defeating the Americans, 4-0, in the World Cup semi-final. Marta, who was twenty-one at the time, truly announced herself to the world at that tournament. She scored twice in that semi-final, but Brazil came up short against Germany in the final. This 2011 Brazilian team has another chance, and the road was always going to go through the United States at some point. Clearing that hurdle in the quarter-finals would go a long way toward Brazil capturing its first Women's World Cup.

Meanwhile, the Americans were fighting off the wrong side of history. In five World Cups and four Olympics to this date, they had never finished worse than third in a major tournament. They were champions at five of those nine events. Many players on this 2011 team also remembered the bitter, embarrassing defeat they suffered to Brazil in 2007, including how the Brazilians celebrated.

FIFA had inexplicably arranged for Brazil and the US to stay in the same hotel around that 2007 semi-final. US player folklore tells a story of a tense scene that saw the Brazilians return to the hotel lobby celebrating and playing the drums in the faces of the devastated Americans who were being consoled by family members. Much like Norway's 'train' celebration in 1995 burned into the memories of that American team which lost in the semi-final, the 2007 Brazilian lobby celebration served as constant motivation for US players of this generation.

At this moment in 2011, however, it felt like a nightmare repeating. The Americans are down a goal and down a player. The tension in Dresden, and back home on the other side of TV sets, is palpable. US players, however, knew what they needed: One. More. Chance.

To understand the moment that changed everything for the United States, one first must understand how the moment came into existence. Brazil clung to its one-goal advantage as the clock ticked toward the 120-minute mark in extra-time. Brazilian players – the men more so than the women – are known for their gamesmanship. Killing the clock is a nuanced art as old as the sport itself. Everyone does it when they are leading a match; Brazilians are just known to be . . . creative.

On this day, that meant faking an injury. Simulating an injury is a tricky and generally frowned-upon act. But how can an opponent question whether someone is truly injured without looking like an awful person?

Counteracting this is stoppage time, soccer's inexact answer to time-wasting. The clock doesn't stop in soccer, but time deemed to be 'wasted' is tracked and then added on to the end of a match. So, in theory, the time is not lost. The subjective nature of the process, however, can mean that a team artful and effective at time-wasting can shave precious seconds or minutes off the game to protect a lead. And stoppage time is kept on the referee's watch, typically out of view of players. At that point in a match, time becomes unknown.

That brings us to the 115th minute of the 2011 USA-Brazil quarter-final. Brazilian defender Erika is laying on the ground in her own penalty area – away from the ball – clutching her lower back and rolling in pain. Television replays show that she dropped to the ground about six seconds after an uneventful play in which she was loosely involved. There's no obvious source of injury. The referee motions for medical trainers to enter the field and then she checks her watch – the unspoken message to the United States that she is keeping track of how much time is lost.

Another motioning of the hand: the stretcher team is brought on and Erika is strapped in and carried off the field, behind Brazil's goal. Within seconds – and with international television cameras following her course – Erika sits up on the stretcher, springs off it and begins jogging, rubbing her back as she rounds the corner flag to head toward midfield and check back into the match. Whistles and jeers pour out from the stands of Rudolf-Harbig-Stadion as fans realise that they appear to have been duped. The high-pitched hum turns to a deeper, louder booing as Erika re-enters the field seconds later, and the displeasure turns to momentary applause as the referee – equally unimpressed with the act – issues a caution to the Brazilian defender. Erika smoothly trots by the upraised arm holding the yellow card, stopping her stride in her own box, a few feet from the scene of the crime. Megan Rapinoe promptly whips the ball in on a corner kick, right toward the head of Erika, and play resumes.

Seconds later, the Americans are awarded a foul 35 yards from goal, and the crowd erupts with a chorus of the distinct 'U-S-A!'

chant. The situation is getting desperate for the Americans, but there's a renewed energy from players and fans alike, inspired by the Brazilians' apparent gamesmanship.

The chants carry on as Carli Lloyd sends the free kick wide of the goal. Mild whistling returns from a pro-US crowd as Brazilian goalkeeper Andreia takes her time putting the ball back into play. The clock ticks toward 120 minutes, and an eerie calm comes over the stadium, the scattered screams echoing off the underside of the roof covering the stands. There's a quiet nervousness among the thousands of Americans on hand.

The electronic board goes up at midfield: three minutes of stoppage time. Three minutes until the United States' worst-ever finish at a Women's World Cup. Brazil has another goal kick – another opportunity to eat away at the clock, which has now passed the 120-minute mark.

'I had two minds going at the same time,' Wambach said. 'I had this one side of me that was just relentlessly unable to accept this defeat as reality. And then I had the other side of me, the saner side, that was like, "How is this happening? We are about to lose."'

'I would like to say that I believed every second that it was in the bag,' Heather O'Reilly said, 'but obviously, when you are past 120 minutes, you start to physically feel sick. And I think that was starting to set in.'

Cristiane collects the ball off an errant touch from US defender Christie Rampone, and she heads to the corner of the field. This is where matches die. Get the ball to the corner, play it off a defender and out of bounds to kill time, repeat. Experienced players go to the corner to kill the clock even if an obvious attempt on goal seems possible. Cristiane is an experienced player.

An important piece of going to the corner to kill the clock, however, is having the patience to stay there. Cristiane appears to be doing everything correctly. But when she gets to the corner and sees that Marta has joined her in the attack, she turns around and plays a low-percentage pass with the outside of her left foot as Rampone challenges her for the ball.

'Wow, I can't believe Christie got away with that foul, because I thought she actually fouled the Brazilian,' Wambach thinks, watching from some 50 yards away.

US defender Ali Krieger intercepts Cristiane's pass and plays the ball to Lloyd, who dribbles on an angle across the field, eluding Brazilian defenders.

'Carli, why are you dribbling the ball so much? The ref is about to blow her whistle. Why are you dribbling it, still? Kick it up to me,' Wambach thinks.

But Lloyd has an open Rapinoe in sight and heavy pressure on her heels. Rapinoe has ample space in front of her, but the clock – one with an unknown number of seconds remaining – continues to tick. 'We really have no time,' she thought.

Wambach continues to wait, impatiently, waving her hand to signal to Rapinoe. Now, the picture is clear to Wambach. Rapinoe has space to serve the ball, and there's only one thing she is going to do: put her head down and hit it.

'Stay onside,' Wambach tells herself.

Rapinoe's eyes drop and her left foot swings through the ball.

'Holy shit, she got all of it,' Wambach says to herself.

That she did. But the odds are still low: Wambach is alone in the box, surrounded by four Brazilian defenders, in addition to the goalkeeper. Rapinoe's service must be perfect. Wambach's positioning must be perfect.

'It was kind of a Hail Mary,' Rapinoe says.

In comes the ball from 30-plus-yards towards the back post to Wambach, the most dominant aerial player in the sport. Four yellow jerseys converge upon the point where the ball might drop. Andreia tracks the ball as well and decides to come off her line, and it's a jump-ball now. Brazilian captain Daiane half-heartedly jumps but barely makes an effort, perhaps realising that her goalkeeper has come to claim the ball or perhaps knowing her positioning wouldn't allow her to reach it, anyway. Andreia takes a few long strides and jumps with both hands reaching for the ball.

Wambach patiently waits. 'Don't. Screw. This up.' Wambach's World Cup hopes flash before her.

Andreia seemingly realises mid-jump that she has miscalculated her effort and begins to reach behind her; she falls horizontally. Daiane's half-jump – while backpedalling – has only made her an additional obstacle for her goalkeeper.

Wambach is already in the right position, right on the line which marks the six-yard-box, the ball attracted to her like a magnet, as she describes it. She jumps vertically, rising to meet the ball as she snaps her head forward and through the ball, sending it into the net.

Goal.

The crowd of fans in Dresden erupts. Wambach sprints to the corner to celebrate, cutting her dramatic slide short as she realises she's headed straight for the concrete walkway. She is joined by her entire team, bench players and all, as they sprint past some Brazilian substitutes warming up and past the stretcher which had just a few minutes earlier carried Erika off the field. One chance: that's all Wambach needed.

At 121 minutes and twenty seconds, the goal is the latest ever scored in a World Cup, men's or women's.

'It was fate that we were meant to score that goal,' Wambach said. 'In that moment, with that kind of emotion, with that kind of pressure, with that kind of timeline, with those kinds of circumstances – being down a man, them going up a goal in extra-time, and us scoring; and we still have to go to penalty kicks – there were just so many things rooting against us. I feel like, of course there was skill involved, but I feel like there was some other energy at play that was forcing us to score that goal, because I really can't explain the sequence of events and how it could come to fruition like it did.'

Years later, the Americans can admit that even their unwavering spirits thought about the ramifications of an early exit as that clock ticked away. Said Rapinoe: 'Honestly, it was probably more relief than excitement in that moment. I was like, "Thank God."'

Shortly thereafter, the full-time whistle blows with the match tied at 2-2, and the two teams head to a penalty-kick shootout – the US amped from their incredible (but still incomplete) comeback, the Brazilians trying to come to terms with what had just happened.

The shootout begins with some irony, as Andreia saves Shannon Boxx's shot, but the kick is retaken because the Brazilian goalkeeper moved forwards off her line: a violation. Solo saves Daiane's effort on Brazil's third spot-kick, and the Americans convert all five of theirs to advance to the semi-finals against France. The most epic comeback in Women's World Cup history is complete.

What followed that day in Dresden was an onslaught of attention on the US women, who became instant heroes back home. The Sunday afternoon kickoff, US time – at the quietest point of the year on the US sports calendar – created a perfect platform for the masses to witness the incredible feat.

But the job was hardly finished. Such dramatic victories which come *before* a championship match create difficult circumstances for teams. They are left drained emotionally as much as they are physically. There is still a semi-final to be played in less than seventy-two hours.

US coach Pia Sundhage calls a team meeting the day after the dramatic victory. It turns out to be more of a group therapy session than anything. Each player shares her personal experience relating to the goal and the game. There are stories of families calling from back home and an overflow of text messages. Each player gets to express outwardly what the moment meant and how things played out in the hours afterward.

'OK, that game is now behind us,' Sundhage says. 'Now we move forward.'

The Americans escaped their semi-final against France with a 3-1 victory despite some rocky moments, advancing to play Japan in the final. The US had already faced Japan three times that year, winning all three meetings. Japan was ranked fourth in the world entering the tournament, but the *Nadeshiko* were not universally viewed as serious title contenders. They had faltered at the group stage in four of the first five Women's World Cups, only reaching the quarter-finals in 1995, when the United States ended their run.

A promising first half for the Americans fails to produce any goals. Lauren Cheney just misses on a close-range attempt, and Wambach smacks a long-range effort off the crossbar. Alex Morgan hits the post a few minutes after half-time before Wambach's diving header is tipped over the bar. US players feel like they should be leading by multiple goals.

Morgan finally breaks the deadlock in the sixty-ninth minute, but Aya Miyama equalises for Japan twelve minutes later. *Extra-time.*

Wambach restores the US lead with a textbook header fourteen minutes into extra-time, and the Americans appear to be on their way to their third World Cup title in six attempts. But Japan's captain, Homare Sawa, equalises with three minutes remaining. Sawa scores off a corner kick as she is running away from goal. Her boot gently grazes the ball to redirect it towards goal from an unlikely angle to produce a goal she would later admit she probably could not repeat. This is the time for *Japan's* hero to shine.*

One last chance for the US – in the 121st minute – is denied by Azusa Iwashimizu, who is sent off for denying a clear scoring

* https://www.youtube.com/watch?v=q87y7WGtVmo

opportunity. This match is headed to penalty kicks. The US fails to convert each of its first three spot kicks, and Saki Kumagai buries the winning penalty kick. Japan are champions.

Slightly conflicting emotions come over the US players. There is heartbreak, of course. None of them are inherently *happy* to see Japan win, but there is also an understanding of the incredible, uplifting story on the other side of the equation. A country devastated by natural disaster has rallied around unlikely sporting heroes. In the end, the Americans were the antagonists in the fairytale.

'I was heartbroken, and it took me a long time to understand why those circumstances ended up the way that they did,' Wambach said. 'And the truth of that matter is that nobody knows. Japan was meant to win that game.

'Our team had something more to learn, and I think that's what the next four years, leading into the 2015 World Cup was: trying to figure out what we needed to learn if we were to get the result that we wanted.

'I'm super grateful, because I probably wouldn't have continued playing after the 2012 Olympics, so I got three more years of playing, because I was still searching for that elusive World Cup championship.'

The 2011 Women's World Cup final was, at the time, the most-watched and highest-rated soccer telecast in ESPN history, drawing an average of over thirteen million viewers.*

Players' eyes were opened to just how important their achievements – even in defeat – were when they arrived home to those

---

* https://tvbythenumbers.zap2it.com/sports/2011-womens-world-cup-finals-espns-most-viewed-and-highest-rated-soccer-match-ever-averaging-13-5-million-viewers/98284/ & https://www.fifa.com/womensworldcup/news/fifa-women-world-cup-germany-2011-sets-new-viewing-records-1477957

mobs of people in Times Square. 'I was like, "Do these people know that we lost?"' Rapinoe recalls.

'It was a very present reminder that there was a bigger thing at play, and that is the growth of women's football,' O'Reilly said.

That dramatic goal in the 2011 quarter-final is the catalyst for everything the US women would build over the following four years as they returned to the final in 2015 – once again against Japan – and reclaimed the World Cup title. The bigger crowds and the increased media attention that surrounded the US team in the years following their 2011 run can be traced back to that incredible week in Germany and, in particular, that one day in Dresden.

That measly crowd in New Jersey for the Americans' World Cup send-off match was the rule, not the exception, at the time. The US played at home twice in May that year in front of crowds of nearly identical sizes. They played 2010 exhibitions in front of embarrassingly empty stadiums: 3,069 fans in San Diego; 4,759 fans in greater Atlanta; 2,505 fans in greater Philadelphia. Even the home leg of their World Cup qualifying playoff couldn't produce a five-digit crowd. The US women were largely afterthoughts in a crowded sports landscape.

But flash to late 2011, after their World Cup run, and the crowd sizes spike dramatically: sixteen thousand fans in Kansas City; eighteen thousand each in Portland, Oregon, and Glendale, Arizona. All thirteen home games that year attracted crowds of ten thousand-plus fans, with four of those being sellouts.

'You really can't look at a point, other than '99, that really propelled women's soccer any more than that, at least in this modern era,' Rapinoe said.

'If that moment doesn't happen – obviously if we lose, but even if we just won that game in normal time and it wasn't all that exciting, we're not here today. And, frankly, I don't think we're anywhere near it.'

Women's Professional Soccer would eventually fold in early 2012. The US women's national team would once again capture attention by way of a dramatic, controversial win, 4-3 over rival Canada in the semi-final of the London 2012 Summer Olympics. Morgan's headed goal in the *123rd* minute was the game-winner en route to a third consecutive gold medal for the United States.

The team was once again in the spotlight, and a new professional league was set to begin in 2013. Morgan, Wambach and company had firmly established themselves as an entertaining team that Americans loved. More media and sponsorship opportunities began appearing for players. US Soccer increased its marketing efforts around the team.

As the 2015 World Cup approached, the difference was night and day: crowds of thirty-five thousand-plus in St. Louis, eighteen thousand in San Jose, twenty-seven thousand in greater LA greeted the US women in their send-off games. Their final match before leaving for Canada was – just as it was before the 2011 World Cup – at Red Bull Arena. The match was a lacklustre, scoreless draw against South Korea. But the crowd this time? A sellout: 26,467. What a difference four years make.

The attention that was thrust upon the US team in the summer of 2011 was bottled and developed over the following four years. More media attention than ever zeroed in on the American women as they ascended upon Canada for the World Cup. And the expectations were clear: go win the World Cup.

England's Golden Girl Arrives

....

If parents of opposing teams had had their way, Kelly Smith would never have made it as a footballer. She'd have never represented her beloved Arsenal, and she'd have never gone on to achieve her dream of playing for her country.

That's because, when playing in a team full of boys, against other boys, she was better than all of them. Parents were embarrassed to see this girl from Watford running rings around their son. You can just picture it: 'She shouldn't be on the pitch; my son can't tackle a girl.'

They'd be right, they couldn't tackle her. Not because she was a girl, but simply because she was too good for them. Despite being asked to leave two local clubs because of the backlash, it didn't stop Smith from pursuing her dream.

She'd play for her beloved Arsenal. She'd achieve the ambition of being a professional playing in America, and she'd accomplish the ultimate dream of pulling on an England shirt. With the exception of her professional stint in the US, all of this was achieved while still a teenager.

Smith would make her debut for England at the age of seventeen 'because there was no youth system in place to progress through,' she says, and would soon become a focal point for opposition head coaches, who could see her talent, even if it did come from underneath an oversized men's England shirt (women didn't have their own kit for a while after).

Smith's first major tournament for her country came in 2001 at the European Championships in Germany, but it was a forgettable one, as they crashed out at the group stage after just a single point from their three games and one goal to celebrate.

But the ultimate aim of her side was to reach a World Cup. England had only been to one of the previous three tournaments held ahead of the 2007 tournament in China, which was in 1995. The team, then coached by Ted Copeland, who was later replaced by long serving coach Hope Powell, were able to qualify out of their group, before being beaten by eventual finalists, Germany.

After the disappointment of the 2001 EUROs, Smith and England's focus turned to qualifying for the 2003 World Cup in China – which would later be moved to the United States due to the breakout of the SARS virus.

England would finish second in their qualification group behind Germany, which would mean going into a four-team play-off to claim the one remaining spot from UEFA's allocation of five teams.

After overcoming Iceland in the semi-final, Hope Powell's side lost a two-legged final to France after 1-0 score lines in both the matches home and away.

England and Kelly Smith would not be going to the World Cup.

'Not going to that World Cup was soul destroying for me, especially knowing what I had witnessed in the USA off the back of them winning the tournament in 1999.

'I remember the backbone of our team had been out. The squad wasn't that strong back then like it is now where we have a vast number of players to pick from. We had a select eighteen to twenty players, and I remember against Iceland that I was out, and I think Faye White and Katie Chapman were out too – three key players out. I hoped and prayed we could qualify, but it wasn't meant to be.'

Smith and her team would have the opportunity to play in a major tournament just two years after the World Cup when, in

2005, England would host its first ever home tournament after winning the bid to host the European Championships. The competition would be held in the north-west of the country, and as hosts, England would not have to go through qualification.

They struggled, and despite seeing some big attendances – most notably in their opening game of the tournament at City of Manchester Stadium (over twenty-nine thousand) – they finished bottom of their group, winning just one match against Finland.

Despite that, Smith was positive about the experience of having hosted a major tournament, especially with the interest from the large crowds that attended.

'The 2005 experience was amazing because we didn't have to qualify for that tournament, and obviously it was hosted in our home country.

'It meant we got to play in front of our home fans and we really wanted to develop the game, and TV coverage was starting to happen, so we really wanted to play well to get people talking about women's football.

'It was great because you'd go to the grounds and you'd be playing in front of fifteen to nineteen thousand, which I think was a record at that time for a women's game. It was a lot of fun to play in.'

Germany would go on to win the tournament, but for Smith and her team, attention had already turned to the 2007 World Cup, with China due to be hosts having had to relinquish hosting in 2003.

The EUROs being held in England may not have seen the team progress deep into the competition, but it had given valuable experience to the players of playing in big matches – with some having never experienced that level before.

For teenagers like Karen Carney and Eni Aluko, and other youngsters including Fara Williams and Anita Asante, the EUROs proved a useful development tournament, even if that wasn't necessarily the primary objective.

One of the issues for many of those players was that the league at home wasn't competitive enough. Smith's Arsenal dominated the women's game before the formation of the FA Women's Super League in 2011, winning six of the seven league titles competed for between the years 2000/2001 and 2006/2007. They also won four FA Cups during that same period. So when it came to international football, it was a baptism of fire for some of those players – even for Smith and her Arsenal teammates.

'It was difficult because you know mentally what is coming from international football,' she said.

'But when you're not playing at that level week in, week out and you're playing some league games that you had won before you'd even walked onto the pitch, it makes that step up more challenging.

'Some of the players would have friendly bets between themselves to see what the scoreline was going to be because that's how it was. There were probably only a few teams you knew you'd get a good game against – Charlton and Everton. You'd get into bad habits when it's too easy. You don't do your defensive work because you can get away with it. But at international level you can't do that. The players knew going into the big games that you had to be switched on, and we made sure of that because we knew the magnitude of the game. The players are fitter and faster at international level, and we needed to adjust to be ready for that.'

But with the English public now having been exposed to women's football on a greater scale on their own doorstep, was there more pressure on England to make their first World Cup in twelve years and build on that momentum?

Not according to Smith.

. 'I wouldn't say more pressure, no. There was more excitement coming off the back of 2005 because we'd played a major tournament in front of our home fans and we wanted more of it. We'd tasted it and we knew we were in for a tough qualification.

'We played well in 2005, but it came a little bit too soon for us. But by qualification for 2007 we felt ready. The campaign was intense because we wanted it so much. Some of us like Rachel Yankey, Faye White, Rachel Brown, those players from that era, had played on the national team for a number of years and had never played at a World Cup. We'd never really had a good qualification campaign, so I think a lot of the senior players were really hungry for that tournament. Even the young players like Karen Carney, Jill Scott and Alex Scott were hungry for success and wanted to embed their place in the squad. It was really competitive.'

If England were to qualify for China, they would have to overcome the team that had denied their passage to the 2003 World Cup: France. Along with the French, Hope Powell's side were drawn with the Netherlands, Austria and Hungary – it was arguably one from three with Austria and Hungary some way behind in their development compared with the other three sides.

This was by no means a last chance for Smith to play at a World Cup, but she would be twenty-eight years old going into the tournament, which for many players, is their peak.

'I was so determined, so driven, so hungry to play in that World Cup,' she said.

'For me the World Cup is the best and biggest tournament in the world. I know people talk about the Olympics, but for me it's always been about the World Cup.

'I'd obviously come off the back of a number of injuries and I'd had my struggles to get back to full fitness, but I felt fit and I wanted to help the team. I knew that I had to play well to ignite the team and to get them on board in believing we could qualify for the World Cup.'

It started well for England in their qualifying campaign, with Smith on target twice in their opening game away in Austria, which they won 4-1. The next match would be a landmark moment for

Smith, who would bag her first hat-trick for England in a record-breaking 13-0 win away in Hungary.

'That was a proud day for me, to score thirteen against any international side, no matter what their level, is never easy. Pretty much everything we hit on target that day, went in. We just pushed for as many goals as we could because we knew that with France being the favourites for the group, it could come down to goal difference. We were thinking we can beat Holland on our day, but France is the tough one. Scoring plenty would put pressure on the other nations.'

A Fara Williams penalty was enough to hand victory to England in the Netherlands, before the grudge match against France arrived, which would be played at Blackburn's Ewood Park – one of the venues for the EUROs in 2005.

Despite bagging eighteen goals in their first three matches, coach Powell had a reputation for approaching stronger nations with more caution.

Understandable in one sense. England didn't want to lose their momentum by suffering defeat at home to their closest rival. But it also meant that attacking opportunities would be fewer and farther between, an approach that did not necessarily suit Smith's game or style of play.

'Hope's approach was always quite defensive going into bigger games, so we always did a lot of defensive work and defensive shape. We'd do the same sessions in the morning and in the afternoon, and a few of the players, especially me, would get a little bit bored of it because football for me was about how many goals you score.

'But I could see where she was coming from because if you're hard to beat, then you don't concede, which means you always have a chance of winning a game. But I always felt that she didn't have a lot of belief in our attacking play, maybe because of some of the players we had, but we were always very defensive.

'I was probably one of those that got told off because I'd switch off from my defensive role, because being a number ten I was attack-minded. So if I wasn't doing my defending in training sessions, I would get yelled out because I had switched off. It was all about being good defensively, and when we got the opportunities in the final third, we had to take them.'

That defensive approach would see England draw 0-0 with France in the game at Blackburn, a result that Smith felt was 'a missed opportunity', especially as the French had lost at home to the Netherlands earlier in qualification. While England remained ahead of their rivals, a win would have given them some breathing space heading into the business end of qualifiers.

Smith was on target in a 4-0 win over Austria, before a 2-0 win at home to Hungary followed, which was only made more comfortable thanks to an injury time goal from defender Alex Scott.

Almost eight thousand fans made their way to Charlton's 'The Valley' Stadium for one of the biggest games in the group, as England's last home game of qualification came against the Netherlands.

When England needed their biggest player, she stood up and delivered. A scintillating hat-trick, which included a wonderful goal of individual class, put England out of sight as they led 3-0 shortly after half-time. The cherry on the icing of the cake was added by forward Rachel Yankey, who added a fourth direct from a free-kick to earn England a crucial win going into the final group match away in France.

'I was pleased with my hat-trick. We were brilliant that day, Holland just had no answer, everything just seemed to click for us.'

It would come down to the final match of the group to determine who would go to the World Cup in China. England, led by their majestic number ten who was winning plaudits and turning heads with her performances. Or France, who had been the party poopers four years earlier, and were driven by one of Smith's former teammates during their time together at the Philadelphia Charge in America's Women's United Soccer Association, Marinette Pichon.

The game was to be played in Rennes, and England only needed a point to progress. The media attention for the game was significantly higher, thanks to the FA flying out a handful of journalists for the fixture to ensure there was ample coverage and interest.

While still not quite the headline act due to the lack of publicity surrounding women's sport – which according to charity Women in Sport, stood at just 7 per cent of coverage in the UK in 2017 – England had made the line-up, and now was their time to shine.*

France were ranked sixth in the world, six places above England in twelfth. They also very much hold the upper hand in terms of previous meetings, having not lost to their opponents in thirty-two years.

It was a wet night in Brittany that welcomed Hope Powell's side, along with a crowd of nineteen thousand, with shouts of 'Allez Les Bleues' ringing around the ground.

'I remember the dressing room, the lay out of the pitch, everything, we only had a small section for our friends and family – you could see where they were because of the red and white, but it was a whole sea of blue from the French fans.

'It was such a positive atmosphere in the dressing room. Even the quieter players were up for it when everyone was teeing the players up.

'I remember standing in the tunnel, puffing my chest out and thinking "we're going to do this, this is our one opportunity to knock France out." I felt some arrogance in my own skin, it was the

* https://www.womeninsport.org/about-us/visibility-for-womens-sport/

weirdest sensation. I didn't necessarily think we'd win, but I didn't think we'd be beaten – I could just sense it.'

Hope Powell's tendency to go defensive against some of the stronger nations would work to her benefit for this fixture, with France taking the ascendency in search of the goal that would break England hearts for a second World Cup qualification in a row.

But knowing they had to take the game to England, left gaps for Powell's team to exploit. It would be an own goal from forward, Hoda Lattaf, who deflected a Yankey free-kick past keeper Sarah Bouhaddi with just under half an hour remaining, that would swing the pendulum heavily in England's favour.

'We were really in the game, creating a lot of chances, but it wasn't happening,' says Smith.

'Then we got the break with the own goal and I remember thinking "We've got the break, we just need to hang on." I remember slide tackling and chasing back, everyone was up for it. You could see the hunger to get into shape, we were so disciplined. We had to stop Pichon, she was the threat and I knew what she could do from my time in Philadelphia.'

England battled on, but a nervy few minutes laid in wait, as substitute Ludivine Diguelman was able to beat Rachel Brown in the England goal to level it up.

Smith knew the last few minutes would be difficult, but that her team had to stand firm.

'They scored in the eighty-eighth minute and I had this sinking feeling in my boots thinking, "Oh my god." I had cramp, my tongue was hanging out and I couldn't think straight because the crowd was so loud. We had to defend for our lives. I think they hit the bar, and then you think it's got to be our time. Eni Aluko hit the post on the counter attack, and then I just remember the whistle went – I just fell to my knees and punched the ground, because we were going to a World Cup. I just didn't want to leave the pitch.'

Over nineteen thousand French fans had been left stunned. They had not only failed to beat England, but they would not be going to the World Cup. The chants of Allez Les Bleus, had been replaced with the sounds of England player celebrations on the field, and by a small section of friends and family in the stands.

Hope Powell told FIFA's website after the game that she was 'delighted it was over,' but that her team had deserved to qualify, especially having finished top of their group, and doing it undefeated.

'We remained unbeaten throughout – that showed the character of the side and I believe there is a lot more to come,' said Powell.

'It's been hard work. It's been a long journey, but it's been a rewarding journey.'*

That rewarding journey had only just begun, with the team now preparing for its first World Cup in twelve years, with a squad that had talented pieces scattered throughout – none more so than Smith.

But all the talent in the world wouldn't be able to compensate for the current state of domestic football in England, with players only training two to three times a week with their club, and having to balance their daily lives with their football.

Hope Powell had moved the game forwards considerably during her time as England Head Coach, taking on more than just her duties with the national team, as she looked to improve standards from the bottom up. Sports psychologists were brought into the England setup, and the number of internationals played over the course of the year increased.

But when players were away with their clubs, she needed to ensure they were doing all the right things to make sure they were ready for China.

* https://www.fifa.com/womensworldcup/news/england-celebrate-france-commiserate-106458

'We were only training a few nights a week with our club, so we had to do extra fitness work by ourselves,' explained Smith.

'So Dawn Scott, the FA's exercise fitness coach at the time, wrote everyone individual fitness programmes and organised for the England players to have regional groups where she'd hire a fitness instructor to deliver the speed and endurance programme that she had developed.

'It would often be us (Arsenal) and Chelsea players doing this at Hertfordshire University, with other groups from clubs in different parts of the country completing Dawn's programme elsewhere.

'The instructor would work us hard and we'd have that session twice a week. We'd just run and be put through our paces to ensure we were at a higher fitness level. We knew we had to be much fitter and stronger for international football. Four minutes of hard work on, a couple of minutes off, and repeat. Just run as hard as you can. We had more meet ups as a team and fitness testing so Hope could see where we were at.'

Meanwhile, Smith's Arsenal side would go on to dominate women's football, not just in England, but in Europe as well in the season leading up to the World Cup, winning an unequalled quadruple that saw them claim the Women's Premier League (now Women's Super League), the Women's FA Cup, League Cup and the Women's UEFA Cup.

Smith bagged twenty-one goals in the league that season and struck twice in the Women's FA Cup Final in front of twenty-five thousand fans at Nottingham Forest's City Ground to help her side claim every trophy they competed for – it was the greatest single season ever seen in women's football in England.

The Arsenal forward would miss the UEFA Cup Final against Umeå of Sweden, due to suspension following a red card in the semi-final, but she was in the form of her life going into the World Cup, and couldn't wait to get out to China.

Of course, conditions in Asia would be quite different from what

England were used to. The humidity and air quality in areas such as Shanghai, would make it difficult for Hope Powell's players, which is why she took them to former Portuguese colony, Macau, to acclimatise.

'We spent two or three weeks in Macau before the tournament to acclimatise because it was a long flight and different temperature,' said Smith.

'We were in a really nice hotel and I remember stepping out and you would literally be sweating getting off the bus and walking to the training pitch.

'You'd have these ice buckets by the field. We'd only train for about twenty minutes, then we'd be over there putting our hands in because of the sensitive point in your wrist. We had towels with ice for the back of your neck as well, but after a couple of days you got used to it. We prepared by playing against some boys' teams, which added some intensity and helped us prepare for what was ahead.'

Beijing was due to host the Olympics the following year and a number of athletes, much like Smith and her teammates, were training in China to adjust to the climate ahead of their pursuit of a gold medal.

She recalls one session in Macau where the England team were training at the local stadium, which they were sharing with a British runner, who was using the track that ran along the outside of the field. That British runner would go on to win Olympic gold medals and world titles, and would become Britain's greatest ever middle-distance runner.

'Mo Farah, before he became the superstar that he is, was staying in our hotel and was using the running track around the pitch. Before we got there, he was running, and then when we finished an hour later, he was still running. We didn't know who he was back then, but we knew he was an Arsenal fan because some of the girls spoke to him at the hotel we were both staying at. It wasn't until years later that we were like, "Oh my god, that was the guy running around the track".'

The World Cup draw in Wuhan earlier in the year had placed England in a difficult group alongside Argentina, Japan and world champions, Germany. If England were going to progress to the knockout stages, they would have to do it the hard way.

But Smith wasn't bothered. She and her team were pleased to be in China, and with the preparation in Macau, and Head Coach Powell's planning, she felt ready to take on the world.

'We were lucky enough that Hope had prepped very well and done a recce, looked at the training facilities and was happy with them.

'She was happy with where the hotel was in Shanghai, which is where our first two games were, and we brought our own chef over because we were told the food was going to be things we weren't used to – like rice for breakfast.

'I remember seeing a duck's head in one of the dishes when we came down for breakfast, but our chef brought out porridge, toast, cereals, eggs, and chicken dishes and pasta for later in the day.

'I know my dad and family members struggled a bit with the food. My dad said he was offered shark's tongue once and he said Karen Carney's mum spent all her time in McDonald's.'

England's first game of the tournament would be in Shanghai against Japan, who themselves were looking to make their mark at a major tournament having lived in the shadow of China during the 1990s.

In midfielders Homare Sawa and Aya Miyama, they had genuine game-changers. But it was Japan's technical ability that was admired by opposition sides, with few teams better at being able to keep the ball and frustrate the opposition.

The two teams would square off at the Hongkou Stadium in Shanghai having seen Germany thump Argentina 11-0 the previous day. All of a sudden, knowing that the world champions had made an early statement, the match took on greater meaning.

Despite Japan's reputation for frustrating the opposition, it was England who started the brighter and created the better chances. The best opportunity fell to forward Eni Aluko, who pounced on a mistake by keeper Miho Fukumoto after she had misjudged a Smith through ball. Unfortunately for England, Aluko dragged her shot wide, which meant the teams would go in scoreless at half-time.

'Mentally it's tough to play Japan as you can have quite a bit of the game without the ball, so you have to be disciplined and sense when to go and press and hope that your teammates go with you. But we had worked on it in training so we were confident. We knew when we got the ball, we had to keep it. As long as we got our ball players on the ball, we had to make sure we didn't give it up too easy, and I think we did that quite well in the first half.'

England would start the second half well with midfielder Katie Chapman seeing a shot blocked within five minutes of the restart, but then five minutes later, disaster.

Japan won a free-kick on the edge of the box and Miyama, their free-kick specialist, was stood over it. She took a few steps back, picked her spot, and was able to fire through England's wall past Rachel Brown – 1-0 Japan, against the run of play.

Big games require big players, especially in times of need, and with less than ten minutes remaining, England's star would not only step up, but would also announce herself to the world.

With the clock ticking down, defender Alex Scott was able to win a ball in the middle of the field, with the ball breaking to Carney, who spotted Smith making a run towards the box, before she fed a pass into her.

Smith, with her first touch, was able to turn her defender Hiromi Isozaki with her back to goal, jink past her and slot the ball past Fukomoto. It was a tremendous piece of skill, a wonderful finish, which was followed by a celebration that saw her take off her left boot – which she had just scored with – and raise it up to the crowd.

'I thought before the tournament that if I score at a World Cup, I want to celebrate – that's what the World Cup is for, it's meant to be fun.

'I thought, "I can't take my top off because Brandi Chastain [US defender who won the 1999 World Cup] has done that," and I wouldn't do it anyway. I thought you know what, I'm going to take my boot off and hold it up, because that's the boot that scored the goal. Then I never thought anymore of it.

'Then when I got the opportunity and the goal went in, that's when I took the boot off. I ran, even though I didn't plan on running. I didn't plan on kissing it, it wasn't planned, I just got lost in the moment. So yeah, I added bits on in that moment.

'But I can see now many years after how that might look, but I don't care because no-one knew my history in the build-up to that dream. Two knee surgeries, broken leg, Achilles tear – I had a lot of time out of the game and being deep and down and depressed with football.

'So for me to get myself out of that in tip-top shape and play in a World Cup, that is all part of my journey, and people didn't know about that, so I don't care if they thought it was arrogant.'

It is well known that Hope Powell was not impressed with Smith's celebration and gave her a telling off after the match, so she will have had mixed feelings once again just two minutes later, when Smith scored her second.

This time, both boots came off after she had broken into the box, fired a left foot shot that was saved by Fukomoto, before smashing in the rebound with her right. Two for England, and two for Smith with just seven minutes to hold out.

England would have some defending to do, and unfortunately, they wouldn't be able to get their first win of the tournament as Miyama would score an even better free-kick than the first one with the last kick of the game.

'I was there in the last minute, thinking we had won. We were playing our first game of the World Cup, and we had won – but that was a silly thing to think.

'Miyama stepped up and scored a wonderful free-kick and it wasn't until years later that I knew it wasn't a fluke, because she did it again so many times.

'I remember feeling deflated after the game. We hadn't lost but we were so close to three points. It was a bit of inexperience giving a free-kick away in the last minute, it was our own undoing. We felt disappointed.'

However disappointed the team might feel, Smith's two goals had ignited conversation amongst people in the world of women's football. Her ability was without question, and she had been heavily tipped to shine in China. Her two goals against Japan were the perfect start.

But she and her teammates would have to pick themselves up and dust themselves off after the last-minute goal, as they would face Germany in their next match, again in Shanghai. Much like their record against France, England would have to end a miserable run against the Germans that had never seen them beat coach Silvia Neid's side before.

After her heroics against Japan, Smith knew – especially in the wake of her boot celebration – that she would be a player the Germans would target.

'Hope sat me aside after and told me, "Don't ever do that again, you're already a target because of the player that you are". I told her I wouldn't do it again, but I thought to myself that I am not sorry for it. In my mind I was thinking, "I've just scored two goals and I am being told off," but I never did it again the rest of my career. But for me, I was always a targeted player so it didn't matter if I did that or not.'

Despite 'a few wallops' from the German defence, a disciplined, resolute and determined performance would see England claim a 0-0 draw against the Germans, which would give them a significant chance of qualification with just Argentina to play in Chengdu, who had already lost to Germany and Japan.

Powell's side would be given an early helping hand after an Argentina own goal, with midfielder Jill Scott adding another before half-time. England would pull away in the second half, despite conceding, to win the match 6-1. Smith would add two more goals to the two against Japan in another positive display, taking her total to four.

Goal one accomplished: England had made it to the quarter-finals, knocking out a competent and talented Japan side in the process. Up next, was a team littered with players familiar to Smith – the USA.

England would move from Chengdu to the northern city of Tianjin, around 1,200 miles away, for the encounter with the 1999 champions, and one of the favourites for the tournament.

'It was probably one team you didn't want to face to be honest. They were one of the powerhouses in the women's game. Looking back at the players they had, they were stacked. They were strong all over and we knew we'd be up against it. We still had players who could hurt the opposition, if we had that luck in front of goal.'

Unfortunately for England, they didn't get that, not just in front of goal, but luck would conspire against them throughout the match.

A close first half saw the teams level at half-time, but the US did inflict one blow on England, which came courtesy of an Abby Wambach elbow to Faye White's nose. Powell admitted the collision had 'shaken up' her defender when speaking after the match.

The second half was settled in a frantic twelve-minute period that saw the USA score three times through Wambach, and midfielders Kristine Lilly and Shannon Boxx, leaving England with an uphill struggle and an almost impossible mission.

Smith had been unable to influence the match due to being closely marked throughout by midfielder, Leslie Osborne. Osborne, who would go on to become a teammate of Smith's in Boston three years later, admitted that her side felt that if they could shut down Smith, then they would shut down England.

She explains:

'Kelly was their most dangerous player so my role was to take her out of the game, not in an injury kind of way, but don't let her be a factor/threat. If we could execute that game plan, we could take care of the rest, and we did.

'But it was incredibly difficult. She is one of the best players I have ever had to play against, let alone track. And I had never followed anyone around before this game so it was a new thing for me, especially at the national team level – let alone in a World Cup.

'I grew up with players marking me all game, so it was crazy that roles were reversed. Having said that, I was willing to do whatever it took to win and have our team be successful. Kelly is crazy talented – on and off the ball. So smart, savvy, technical, creative and her IQ is just at another level. I had to have one of my best games in my career in order to do my job.'

Osborne's marking of Smith had done the job. USA progressed to the semi-finals, and England were going home, 'beaten by the better team,' confessed England's number ten.

It would be back to reality for Hope Powell's players – one weekend playing in front of thousands at a World Cup, to the next, playing in front of a few hundred – if they were lucky – when representing their club.

All of a sudden, that adrenaline rush had evaporated, and Smith admits the players had to re-adjust to being home.

'It was deflating, because you knew that experience was over. We didn't know what to expect coming home.

'I remember playing a league game with Arsenal after experiencing the highest high with England, and there was nobody at the game.

'I was so mad because I had experienced the ultimate, and this is what women's football was about in England. I think a few players took a month to get back to reality, mentally, after experiencing that high.'

It was a situation where players had been brought crashing back to reality, but it was slightly different for Smith, whose four goals in China had attracted a lot of attention. All of a sudden, it wasn't 'Kelly Who,' but 'Kelly Smith the Footballer', the woman who had taken off her boot and raised it to the world.

It attracted attention. Smith was, all at once, a woman in demand. Media were keen to speak to her, including television presenter, Jonathan Ross, who invited her onto his prime-time chat show to talk about the World Cup.

'It was a bit surreal really. There were media opportunities like the one with Jonathan Ross. Jonathan had watched the World Cup and the England games. I wasn't sure about going on his show, I was nervous. I didn't want him to make fun of me or women's football – I didn't want to go on and be ridiculed.

'I had that conversation with him in the green room before and told him not to make me look stupid. I think he could have taken it further than he did, at that time the joke was always about whether players shower together or change shirts after games. But I enjoyed the majority of the interview.'

The 2007 World Cup was a defining moment for Kelly Smith. She'd been banned from her boys' teams as a young girl. She'd battled with career-threatening injuries, depression and the struggle of being in the spotlight.

But she would go on to achieve even more, including firing her England side to the final of the European Championship in 2009, and being voted as a finalist for the Women's World Player of the Year (Ballon d'Or).

But with that added profile, comes attention. And for a woman who expressed so much confidence on the pitch, off it, it was something that she would have to adjust to for the rest of her career.

'I knew I was gifted with a special talent, and I worked hard to develop that. I had to fine tune it and learn to play. I studied the game on how I could be better, and I knew that I was the best player on the team. I knew if I played well, others would play well too. I knew I could make my teammates play better and I enjoyed that because I was helping them to play better.

'I never thought about being a great, never, ever. I just wanted to play at a World Cup because that was the dream. I wanted to show what talent I had and what I could do, and the only way to do that is at a World Cup, because everyone is watching.

'I never thought about making a name for myself, I just wanted to show what I could do, live the dream and have fun. From the age of five or six, it was my dream to be on that stage.'

A Hat-Trick and a
Worldwide Movement

....

The game clock struck 15:00 when the ball left Carli Lloyd's right foot. The American had already scored twice and her team was three goals ahead of Japan in a match that was playing out more like a training-ground exhibition than a Women's World Cup final.

Some fans had yet to settle into their seats at BC Place in downtown Vancouver, but the game's result was already decided. The United States women's national soccer team, meeting Japan in a third straight major-tournament final, scored three times in the opening fourteen minutes – an unprecedented blitz even by their historically dominant standards. Lloyd, already twice the Olympic gold-medal hero in her career, was responsible for two of those goals. The US legend had erased the memory of an average first few games of the 2015 World Cup – for her and her team – and her move from a more traditional midfield role to, by all intents and purposes, a forward role was among the key changes that unlocked the potential of this talented American team. The change was the springboard to Lloyd's typically clutch late-tournament performances, those which would be the most tired of clichés if she didn't keep delivering them – but she just kept on delivering. She scored the gold-medal clinching goals at the 2008 and 2012 Olympics. This day was yet another to remember.

A quarter-hour into this fairytale match, Lloyd outdid herself again. After recovering possession inside her own half of the field,

Lloyd poked the ball around her defender with the slightest of touches and moved into open space at the centre of the field. A quick glance from nearly 60 yards away showed that Japan goalkeeper Ayumi Kaihori was well off her line. Lloyd, known for her excessive training habits, had practised shooting from midfield for years. Instinctively, the decision had already been made: go for it.

Lloyd lined up the most audacious and improbable of shots just as the ball crossed midfield – her left foot planted in Japan's half of the field; her right foot swinging through across the centre line, as if it were single-footedly smashing through a glass wall. Nobody had scored a goal from that distance in a Women's World Cup final. Nobody had scored a hat-trick in the first sixteen minutes of a final. Nobody had scored a hat-trick in a Women's World Cup final, *period*.

So, as Lloyd launched the ball from under the shadows of BC Place, high into the air and through the patch of sunlight peeking through the partial roof, towards Japan's goal, time appeared to slow down inside the stadium. The thick and hazy air from wildfires blazing across British Columbia only added to the illusion that the ball was somehow travelling slower in that moment. There was a collective feeling – in the press area wedged between fans, on the sideline among the players and training staff:

NO. WAY.

Just four seconds later, it was reality. Kaihori stumbled backwards to recover towards her goal, perhaps struggling to track the ball in the blinding, late afternoon light of the July sun. Her reaching right hand could only slightly redirect the ball, which bounced off the inside of the goalpost and into the net. *Four-nil, USA.*

Lloyd sprinted around the field pumping both index fingers up and down. Countless times throughout her preparations, she had visualised her championship moment, but the audacity of this particular goal – the scoreboard lighting up 4-0 after just sixteen minutes – surprised even her.

Lloyd's longtime trainer and mentor, James Galanis, had predicted that she would score a hat-trick in the final. He drafted a text message that morning to tell her as much, but deleted it before pressing send, fearing Lloyd might become *too* focused on hitting the three-goal mark. She had already been sleepless with anticipation in the nights prior to that decisive match in Vancouver.

Galanis did, however, send Lloyd the usual game-day email. 'You are once again going into this final as the best Carli Lloyd there ever was,' it begins, noting that Lloyd is 'on the brink of shocking the world again.' Twice the scorer of the gold-medal clinching goal at the Olympics, it was time to make the World Cup hers, the email read. Lloyd did exactly that.*

Her hat-trick powered the United States to a 5-2 victory, earning the programme a record third Women's World Cup title. The tournament had its hero. It had its defining moment. Lloyd's goal was the rare type that makes people remember where they were when they witnessed it. Whether among the fifty-three thousand-plus in the stadium in Vancouver, or part of the 26.7 million people watching on television in the US – a record for a soccer match in the country – the memory is enduring. Lloyd's goal is forever etched in history.

Yet, in many ways, the moment was a blip on a wide-ranging plot of data points around this World Cup. Lloyd's on-field brilliance and the United States' magical title run punctuated a much deeper movement taking place off the field, a movement which began well ahead of the tournament kicking off in the quiet city of Edmonton, and a movement which only gained momentum in the aftermath of the Americans' victory. This final – this championship – was merely the start.

*   *   *

* https://sportsworld.nbcsports.com/predicting-carli-lloyd/ – my original reporting; Lloyd also published this email in her book, a year later.

The fight began over two years earlier. Abby Wambach, the face of this generation of US players and the soon-to-be world-record goal-scorer – man or woman – had been quietly gathering allies in 2013 to take on her toughest opponent yet: FIFA.

Canada earned the right to host the 2015 Women's World Cup without opposition. Zimbabwe, the only challenger in the final stage of the bidding process, pulled its bid shortly before FIFA decided. That left Canada to bring the Women's World Cup back to North America for the third time – and, for the first time, play the tournament on artificial turf.

That crumb-rubber filled, green-plastic bladed surface would become the singular talking point of the entire build-up to the 2015 Women's World Cup. The players had over two years as a runway to fight for change, a timeframe which Wambach declared, when she first went public in March 2013, 'enough time . . . to get the right people in charge so that this doesn't happen.'

The issue was and remains divisive: players argued that artificial turf caused more injuries than natural grass, that joints endured harder impacts, turf tore up skin and on-field temperatures reached dangerous heights on artificial turf; they argued that the ball bounced differently and skipped faster. And they did so through traditional media and their own large social media networks, posting photos of turf burns on their legs. The game was just different on turf, they said. The powers that be – FIFA, the sport's world governing body, and Canada Soccer, the 2015 hosts – pointed out that scientific studies were either anecdotal or decidedly inconclusive. Turf – especially with technological advancements – was just as safe as natural grass, they said.

But the heart of the argument for players was simple: this was about equality. The men would never be asked to play the World Cup – the pinnacle of the sport, held only once every four years – on artificial turf. And, indeed, when Canada hosts *men's* World Cup games in 2026 as part of a joint-tournament with the US and Mexico, it will host them on natural grass. No senior men's World Cup has ever been played on artificial turf.

'We've worked so hard as female athletes – not only here in the United States, but internationally – to grow the game and in my opinion, I think this is taking a step back,' Wambach said in March 2013. 'All of the men's international players around the world would argue the same point. A lot of these guys will not play on an artificial surface because it is an injury-prone surface and I don't blame them.'*

Tension built over the next year, and in July 2014, a group of approximately forty players from national teams around the world – headlined by Wambach – obtained legal counsel. The group wrote to FIFA and Canada Soccer arguing that the use of 'a second-class surface is gender discrimination that violates European charters and numerous provisions of Canadian law, including human rights codes and the Canadian Charter of Rights and Freedoms.'

FIFA and Canada Soccer initially kept low profiles on the topic publicly, which gave players the upper hand in the public relations battle. Celebrities from Tom Hanks to Kobe Bryant got behind the women's players as public opinion tipped heavily against the bureaucrats who were forced to defend themselves. Victor Montagliani, at the time the president of Canada Soccer, in September 2014 denied accusations of systemic sexism, calling them 'nothing but misinformation and typical hyperbole.'†

By October 2014, the group of players turned to the Ontario tribunal, feeling that they hadn't made any progress in discussions

---

* https://equalizersoccer.com/2013/03/22/wambach-world-cup-not-the-place-for-artificial-turf/ – my original reporting

† https://www.sportsnet.ca/soccer/montagliani-turf-not-a-result-of-discrimination/

– or lack thereof – with FIFA despite threatening legal action. They argued that the differential treatment of the women's tournament constituted a violation of the Ontario Human Rights Code. By that point, however, the ample time to make changes, which Wambach had cited eighteen months prior, had seemingly passed. The World Cup was just around the corner. Even if players were granted their expedited hearing – and even if the Human Rights Tribunal of Ontario would have had the power to enforce changes to a tournament played across the entirety of Canada – there wasn't enough time to change the logistics of a major world sporting event, organisers argued. Players' legal counsel thought otherwise, having maintained contact with the world's leading experts on grass. But the players' delay in bringing the matter to legal proceedings was cited, in part, as why their request for an expedited hearing was rejected. Canada won the bid to host the 2015 World Cup back in 2011, at which time it was made clear that the tournament would be played on turf. FIFA approved that decision in March 2013. Now, the tournament was only seven months away.*

In some ways, though, the players got what they wanted. The monumental task of taking on FIFA and forcing multi-million-dollar changes to a major sporting event was always a longshot, even if players tried everything in their attempts to handle things the 'reasonable' way, through 'good-faith negotiations'.

Of greater importance for Wambach – who used the latter years of her career and her post-playing career to champion equality – and the rest of the players, was the future. At a certain point during the

---

* https://equalizersoccer.com/2014/10/01/players-officially-file-lawsuit-against-fifa-csa-over-artificial-turf-at-2015-womens-world-cup/ & https://equalizersoccer.com/2014/09/05/fifa-canada-victor-montagliani-respond-latest-2015-world-cup-turf-accusations/ – my original reporting

process in 2014, players came to the realisation that they were unlikely to succeed in getting the 2015 Women's World Cup played on grass. When, exactly, that was depends on who you talk to. But they knew that simply going away quietly might unintentionally send FIFA the message that they could get away with using women's soccer's biggest stage as a laboratory.

So, the players fought. They kept fighting even as the draw to determine groups and matches took place on 5 December 2014. The day typically reserved as the unofficial start of six months of celebration and anticipation leading into the World Cup was instead swallowed up by this ongoing turf war. The enduring image of that day in Ottawa was of then FIFA Secretary General Jérôme Valcke becoming heated on stage and on international television as he fielded questions not about teams, games or the typical fluff about how wonderful the tournament would be, but instead about the controversy of artificial turf.

'If anyone is saying that the use of the artificial pitch is a question of discrimination, it's nonsense. It has nothing to do with discrimination,' he said.*

Wambach would state after a January 2015 meeting with FIFA officials that decisions were set in stone, but she would also later note that FIFA officials had promised her that there would never again be a Women's World Cup played on artificial turf. That's hardly a binding contract, but it was clear that this type of battle for equality was going to be necessary, whether in 2015 or down the line. Around that same time, FIFA announced an increase in prize money for the Women's World Cup, which was a small victory that at least appeased players. Women's players had long been told to be

---

* https://equalizersoccer.com/2014/12/05/jerome-valcke-world-cup-turf-discrimination-nonsense-fifa-prize-money-goal-line-technology/ – my original reporting

thankful for what they had. The two years of battling the bigwigs over what women's players felt was, morally and legally, gender discrimination, proved to be the exposition to the approaching tidal wave of the fight for equal rights.

Seventy miles north of the US-Canada border at Interstate-29 in North Dakota sits Winnipeg, a mundane city at the southern tip of Manitoba. It's 8 June, and the city has been overrun by thousands of Americans decked out in red, white and blue. The US women's national team is opening its much-anticipated World Cup campaign here at this multipurpose venue. That it is primarily a field used for the pigskin type of football – and that it is set on the campus of the University of Manitoba – hardly screams, 'WORLD CUP!' But the flock of American fans largely responsible for filling the stadium to capacity provides the atmosphere to be expected at a big event.

Twelve minutes into the match, Megan Rapinoe collects the ball and spins toward goal, her unmistakable bleach-blonde hair popping out as a dot in the middle of four all-navy Australian jerseys which appear to form a perfect diamond around her. Rapinoe's shot deflects off a defender and skips into the back of the net. One-nil. The crowd is buzzing.

'U-S-A! U-S-A! U-S-A!'

What would become the defining chant of this 2015 Women's World Cup would score no points for originality, but it was a rallying cry for an American fan base which largely made the US a 'home' team in Canada. It is some wonder how the tournament might have played out under the exact same scenario – same teams, same groups, same games – but in a different country. The US women faced significant adversity, but unlike in past tournaments abroad, where their travelling contingency of fans was relatively small, they had the herd of American Outlaws fan group to inject life into them at every stop along the way. Six of the United States' seven matches on their march to victory were played in cities easily accessible by car from the US – Winnipeg and Vancouver (twice each), Ottawa and Montreal. US midfielder Heather O'Reilly would later describe the World Cup's proximity as the perfect scenario: the feel of a home World Cup without the pressure of being hosts.

Fifteen minutes after Rapinoe's opening tally of the tournament, Lisa De Vanna equalises for Australia. A lesser but considerable roar from the crowd serves as a reminder that the Americans would not enjoy exclusively partisan crowds – if for no other reason than Wambach and company made themselves public enemies to many Canadians in their long battle against artificial turf. Plenty took the accusations personally, another example of brash Americans taking shots at a rival.

Christen Press and Rapinoe would each score in the second half to secure a 3-1 victory for the US, and it was embattled goalkeeper Hope Solo who was equally responsible for the result. Australia outplayed the US for large portions of the match, only to be denied by spectacular saves from Solo. Victory papered over flaws for the United States.

A scoreless draw with Sweden four days later in the same stadium frustrated the Americans, in large part because of how predictable it was. A series of mind games in pre-match press conferences set the table as US players faced off against their former coach, Pia Sundhage, who was now in charge of her native country after guiding the US to a pair of Olympic gold medals. The Americans would narrowly defeat Nigeria four days later in Vancouver to finish atop Group D and advance to the round of sixteen. Part one of the job – winning the group – was complete, but it wasn't pretty.

'The play wasn't flowing well and that obviously showed in the group play,' O'Reilly observed, reflecting years later. 'We were getting the results, but nobody felt great about the football that we were putting out.'

'It was a team of much experience,' Rapinoe says in reflection, 'but there were quite a bit of new pieces happening. The experience of the players sort of dragged us along and was able to sort of keep the ship right. But it was sort of almost a duelling of two styles, half in one style and half in another style. We were trying to figure that out for ourselves.'

This was the first such round of sixteen in the history of the women's event, which in 2015 was expanded from sixteen to twenty-four teams. Increasing the number of teams in the World Cup is a necessity for the growth of the women's game, and in 2015, it allowed eight countries – one-third of the field – to appear in a Women's World Cup for their very first time. One such country was Colombia, the Americans' opponent in the round of sixteen.

Frustration within this US team was outwardly evident throughout the build-up to the World Cup, and some of the small cracks in confidence were playing out under the spotlight in Canada at the early stages of the tournament.

Jill Ellis took over as full-time head coach of the team in May 2014 following the unceremonious ousting of Tom Sermanni. The Americans placed seventh at the annual Algarve Cup in Portugal in March 2014, their worst finish at the tournament in history. The headline result was a 5-3 loss to Denmark, the most goals the US women ever conceded in a single match. Losses, combined with a stylistic difference in management – Sermanni is a laid-back players' coach, and the US women's national team is known as the most cut-throat environment in the sport – and the ongoing roster rotation caused some players to lose confidence in the direction of the team. That feeling worked its way to the upper levels of US Soccer and Sermanni, who had only been in the job for just over a year, was fired in the hours after a 2-0 exhibition win over China outside of Denver. The team was due to fly to San Diego for a second game against China four days later.

'I was completely blindsided,' Sermanni said in the aftermath. He continued: 'To put it in a nutshell, they just felt that the way I was managing the team wasn't working.' Gulati denied rumours of a player revolt in the days that followed, but conceded that senior players were always consulted about coaching changes.

Ellis took over as interim coach and was announced as the permanent coach just over a month later. Whereas Sermanni tinkered, sacrificing some results in order to test out and vet new players, Ellis' instructions from the federation – and the players – were clear: *This is the group with which you are going to win the World Cup.* Senior players had spoken of the need for a coach to 'steer us in the right direction' and 'blend the old [players], blend the new [players].' Ellis – who would enjoy much more freedom to make decisions after the 2015 triumph – obliged. Player management was as important a task as anything.*

Wambach turned thirty-five years old just four days before the 2015 World Cup kicked off. Citing a gruelling career, and that she knew her body best, Wambach decided to sit out the 2015 National Women's Soccer League season. She would play only for the US; all of her attention was focused on winning the World Cup title which had eluded her legendary career. It was the sole reason she was still playing at this point, having been denied in the final of the last Women's World Cup. Those motives were sound, but the approach was relatively unheard of. She was going to prepare for the biggest tournament of her career by . . . not playing?

* https://www.si.com/node/2013286 & https://soccer.nbcsports.com/ 2014/04/11/uswnt-china-result-coaching-search-underway-ellis-riley-waldrum-gustavsson/ – the latter is my original reporting

Ellis had the delicate task of managing the situation. The very act of being complicit to the decision threatened to question the coach's authority. But it wasn't as if Wambach's place on the team was ever in jeopardy.

At least that matter pertained to what was happening on the field. There was also the unending attention being placed on Hope Solo, who had been accused one year earlier of domestic violence by her half-sister and nephew. The court process had drawn out, and new details of Solo's arrest were released the day before the US women were to open their World Cup campaign against Australia. That ESPN report, stating that Solo was combative toward police during her 2014 arrest, brought a new wave of questions and specu- lation to the US camp in Winnipeg. Ellis spent the day before her team's opening World Cup match deflecting questions about Solo, distractions and hypothetical discipline.*

Behind the scenes, the dynamics between the team and media spiralled from typically pleasant to a tense, antagonistic relation- ship. And while the team was winning, it was hardly convincing in doing so. Pressure began building internally and externally. Ellis spoke constantly – almost daily – of keeping her team 'in the bubble', a phrase which meant different things for different players. Some read the headlines; others disconnected from social media entirely. This was the largest press contingency and the most amount of attention on the US women sicne 1999 and the dynamics had changed. The players turned to each other to insulate themselves and focus on the soccer.

'There is something special about team environments during big tournaments,' O'Reilly said, looking back on her fourteen-year

* http://www.espn.com/espn/otl/story/_/id/12976615/detailed-look- hope-solo-domestic-violence-case-includes-reports-being-belligerent -jail

international career. 'You are playing card games and board games. You don't really do that at any other time in your life except for during those big tournaments. There is an emphasis that this is a really stressful time, so let's stay together.

'So, I think we did a really good job of that, but to say that we didn't know that people were having doubts about our team would be a lie. We felt it internally, and we certainly know that there was commentary about it. But I think that it wasn't breaking us; it was a totally normal amount of stress. And we also know that as female players, if we want to be treated as equals, we need to be able to take that as well, if we're not performing well. I think we just saw it as part of it. Yeah, if you're not playing well as a team and you're scrapping by results, yeah, we want to hear that, actually. It's harsh, but you don't want everything to be fluffy and rainbows and butterflies if it's not. It's just inauthentic.'

Externally, the biggest red flag for the United States' title hopes happened four months prior to the World Cup, in France. The Americans opened the year with a stiff test against fellow World Cup contenders France, and they were played off the park. They lost 2-0 on that blustery February day in the seaport town of Lorient, but the score might as well have been double. Final statistics suggested a relatively even match, but the French exposed the US – particularly in wide areas of the field. The Americans looked far from the world's top-ranked team, and France continued its semi-annual tease of looking like the best team in the world *before* a major tournament, only to choke in the moment.

Fast-forward four months, and these events appeared to triangulate. Colombia advanced to the knockout round of the 2015 World Cup in large part due to a 2-0 victory over France in the group stage – unequivocally the most shocking result in Women's World Cup history. This Colombia team of relative nobodies outplayed world power France – which looked like a better team than the US heading into the World Cup.

Now, it was the Americans' turn to avoid disaster. Colombia entered the match with swagger. Star forward Lady Andrade – who made headlines at the 2012 London Olympics for sucker-punching Wambach – set the tone by sending a warning shot through media before the match.

'They belittle us,' she said of the Americans. 'They think we're a team they're going to walk all over and it will be an easy game for them. We're going to beat them since they like to talk so much.'

Two days after that report, Lady Andrade's words hung over the stadium in Edmonton. The two teams entered half-time scoreless, with the Americans frustrated by the score, their play, and the two cautions issued. Megan Rapinoe and Lauren Holiday each received yellow cards in the first half, meaning they would both be suspended for the next match – if the US even advanced. With forty-five minutes gone, there was a genuine feeling that Colombia's spunk and the Americans' unshakeable lethargy could be the ingredients for another historic upset.

Two minutes after half-time, however, Colombia goalkeeper Catalina Perez was ejected for her tackle on US forward Alex Morgan, and the underdogs would have to play the rest of the match down a player. The US was awarded a penalty kick, which Wambach stepped up to take. Surely this was the beginning of the end for the feel-good Colombia story. But Wambach sliced her left-footed kick wide, and the game remained scoreless. Morgan ended the Americans' angst with a goal a few minutes later, and Carli Lloyd stepped up to take a second penalty-kick – one she converted – as the US gutted out an ugly, 2-0 victory over Colombia. The Americans were through to the quarter-finals in Ottawa, where they would face old rival China. But they were at an inflection point: what had sufficed as just enough to get by wasn't going to be enough to win a World Cup – and they knew it.

One of the wider myths of the 2015 Women's World Cup is that Jill Ellis lucked into the necessary changes which would propel this US team from its slumber to World Cup champions. It is true that Rapinoe and Holiday were suspended for that quarter-final match against China; they could not have played even if Ellis wanted them to. But within the team – Ellis, her staff and players – there was an understanding that change was necessary and inevitable. That Colombia match served as the wake-up call, one which many argue should have come earlier in the tournament. Change was happening, and now Ellis needed to make the *right* changes.

Against China, the US coach inserted midfielders Morgan Brian and Kelley O'Hara for the suspended Holiday and Rapinoe and swapped forward Amy Rodriguez into the lineup in place of Wambach, who would not start for the rest of the tournament. Rodriguez brought mobility which Wambach lacked, and O'Hara was the sparkplug of energy that the team needed to play on the front foot. Brian would sit deeper to allow Lloyd to push higher up the field. Lloyd scored the game's only goal that day, and although 1-0 hardly reads as dominant, the US out-shot an ultra-defensive China team 17-6. The difference was clear between this and the preceding performances. The US had turned a corner.

Four days later, in Montreal, the Americans met Germany in the semi-finals. Each powerhouse had eyes on becoming the first programme to claim three Women's World Cup titles. The US won the inaugural tournament in 1991 as well as the 1999 edition on home soil; the Germans are the only team to win back-to-back titles, in 2003 and 2007. What played out that late-June evening in Montreal was a combination of skill and fortune – the sort of recipe called for in every run to a World Cup triumph.

Julie Johnston was one-quarter of an American defensive unit which, along with Solo in net, was as important a factor as any in the Americans winning the 2015 Women's World Cup. The US would fall mere seconds short of setting a record for the longest single-tournament shutout streak – 540 minutes, held by Germany – in tournament history. For all the concerns about the poor attacking play early in the tournament, the defence was unquestionably otherworldly.

It was the fifty-ninth minute of the semi-final against Germany when controversy fell in favour of the United States. Johnston struggled to track a long, high ball which looped over her head under the roof of the Olympic Stadium, and as Alexandra Popp gained superior positioning inside the penalty box, Johnston stuck out her left arm, dragging down the German attacker. It was a clear penalty and, by the letter of the law, should have been an ejection for preventing a clear and obvious goal-scoring opportunity. But referee Teodora Albon presented a yellow card – not a red card – to an emotional Johnston, and the US had a lifeline. Celia Sasic stepped up to the spot for Germany. *Thud.* Sasic pushed her right-footed kick wide, to her left, and it bounced off the advertising boards behind the goal. No US red card. No goal for Germany.

A penalty at the other end of the field four minutes later gave the US its own opportunity from the spot, one which Lloyd would convert. O'Hara came off the bench in the second half and added an insurance goal for the US in the eighty-fourth minute, scoring on what looked like a flying karate kick, one which sent the heavily pro-American crowd into deafening decibel levels, the roar pinging off the concrete and steel of the four-decade-old indoor stadium. The Americans were headed back to the Women's World Cup final.

What became much easier to see, in retrospect, was that 2015 was a platform for so much more than the United States women's soccer team continuing to dominate its sport. The tournament was about more than just great goals and memorable upsets.

'It was a moment that gave hard results to the things that we had been feeling,' Rapinoe said. Players took notice of the team's rising popularity, the increased commercial opportunities and the bigger crowds after the 2011 World Cup.

'It was kind of that solidifying moment that this is a bona fide operation. Let's everybody – federation, media, players, sponsorship companies – let's everybody get a lot more organised and business-savvy about all of this, so everybody can benefit a lot more.'

The 2015 FIFA Women's World Cup was about fighting. It wasn't just about the fight for natural grass – a public battle of words which would continue throughout the tournament. (During the group stage, Wambach went as far as to say that the US would have been scoring more on natural grass.) It was about fighting for equality; victory for the US, which featured several openly gay players, came just over a week after the US Supreme Court ruled that gay marriage is a right protected by the US Constitution.

It was a fight for equal pay, one which carried on in the wake of 2015 as the American women sought a new collective bargaining agreement with US Soccer. They wanted equitable pay – something closer to what the men were paid. The US men's national team operates under a separate collective bargaining agreement and players are paid each time they receive call-ups; the women have long held yearly contracts which see them paid set rates rather than on a per-game basis.

But the numbers still didn't add up. Many women's national team players were still earning modest salaries. FIFA World Cup prize money – out of US Soccer's control, but very much part of the players' gripes – added fuel to the fire. The US women split $2 million between them for winning the 2015 World Cup; the US men earned $9 million for losing in the round of sixteen of the 2014 World Cup. There's a vast difference in the revenues those two events generate, but domestically, the US women have surged in popularity – and in commercial value – at a time the US men spiralled to rock bottom, failing to qualify for the 2018 World Cup. On the field and in the financial books, the tides shifted drastically.

So, as collective bargaining dragged on, the US women filed a gender discrimination complaint with the US Equal Employment Opportunity Commission in March 2016. This came nearly two months after the US Soccer Federation asked a federal court to force the US Women's National Team Players Association to honour the no-strike clause in the previous agreement; US Soccer would be granted that in June.

Over a year after the US women's players first informed the federation that they were seeking a new deal, a collective bargaining agreement was ratified. The US women successfully negotiated for increased wages and improved professional standards, including better travel conditions and a say in what sort of venues the team would play matches. (The latter was prompted, in part, by Megan Rapinoe tearing her ACL on a subpar grass practice field in Hawaii, which led to US players boycotting the final game of their 2015 World Cup victory tour as they shared photos on social media of the artificial turf at Aloha Stadium.) Base salaries increased by about 30 per cent under the new agreement, and improved bonuses mean players can earn six figures between salaries for club and country. Per diems were returned to being equal to that of the men.

'Our women's national team has always been fighting for more – for more respect, for equal pay – and because of that, that has allowed so many of us who have played and who are still currently playing, to have confidence in the beliefs that we have about what is happening in the world outside the lines of our game,' Wambach said.

'I think that 2015 was a beautiful moment, a confluence of time between gay marriage being recognised and us winning and giving us a platform. Because we have had success fighting for more equal rights for people, because we have had personal success at fighting for better pay inside the lines of our own job, we realise that we have a responsibility to fight for every other marginalised group out there. And I think that 2015 was such a unique, beautiful moment – especially leading into the presidential election in 2016 – that allowed women to create brands for themselves.

'There are players, outside the lines, that go into the social justice realm, and I think that that is such a beautiful and unique story. You don't necessarily see a lot of male – I know LeBron [James] is big in the social justice world – but you don't see a lot of male athletes that are getting their heels so dug into things that are outside the lines of their sport and into the more social mainstream of the way that our culture sees social issues. So, I feel proud that that is a legacy that I have left behind.'

What followed that 2015 Women's World Cup was a belief that women's soccer, women's sports – women everywhere – were, more than ever, ready to fight for equality. Norway in late 2017 became the first federation to grant equal – not equitable, but completely equal – pay to both its men's and women's national teams. New Zealand followed suit in 2018 with the same achievement. Denmark's women's team boycotted a World Cup qualifying game over a dispute with its federation regarding compensation and working conditions. Women's players began fighting for better conditions in traditionally machismo countries, like Argentina.

The 2015 Women's World Cup was a coming of age for women's soccer. It was the crest of the wave that is the movement toward an inclusive future, and it played out both on and off the field. The US women recognised their growing platform as the most high-profile women's sports team on the planet, and they used it to take on inequities for themselves and the generations ahead.

They also owned the moment in Canada as champions. Carli Lloyd immortalised herself with a hat-trick in the final. That moment will forever live in history. Those which followed – the subtext to the progress on display in Canada in 2015 – continue to be written.

Australia's Kids are Alright

The Matildas. For the majority of those that follow women's football, it is a name now synonymous with Australia's national team.

But for nearly two decades Australia's women's national team toiled away in the shadows. It took a 1994 television competition run by Australian broadcaster SBS to bring the team into the light. SBS helped give the team an identity, when the Australian Women's Soccer Association enlisted its help in coming up with a name for the team when it became eligible for government funding.

Women's football in Australia has a long history dating back to the 1920s in Brisbane, Queensland. The first matches saw the 'Reds' and 'Blues' do battle in the suburban grounds and the game took off until the worldwide ban set in. However, fifty years later the game was revived, with Australia forming one of the first national teams in 1974.

Despite its long history, the women's side of football thrived in the dark with no support from the Australian Federation. The turning point for the women's game was the introduction of women's football as an Olympic sport for the 1996 Games in Atlanta. With Sydney successful in bidding for the Games in 2000, football qualified for government funding. While there was a men's programme in place since the 1980s, there was no such programme for the women's team.

Tom Sermanni, who would go on to coach the Matildas in two different stints, was working for Australia's Institute of Sport at the time, and was approached about starting up a women's programme ahead of the Sydney 2000 Olympics, to put a more robust structure in place to support the women's team.

'I had been coaching at the Institute of Sport in the men's programme and they approached me about starting a women's national team programme,' he said.

'It would have funding for some coaches and a youth programme as well. So that is when it started.'

While the men's national team had held the moniker 'Socceroos' since the 1970s, the women's side had little presence in Australia's sporting landscape. To generate publicity and interest, SBS put the call out to the Australian public to suggest a name that could be used to identify the team. The shortlisted names were then put to a poll for people to vote for their favourite.

'I remember driving from Sydney to Canberra in the rain with a mobile phone in my car the size of a brick, and that's when I got a call with the result of the most popular name, which was the Matildas,' recalls Sermanni.

And thus, the Matildas were born.

The genius of the modern-day Matildas coincided with another re-birth for Australia when in 2005, Football Federation Australia (FFA) was created, merging the men's and women's game under one umbrella.

The first major decision for the FFA was to apply for the federation to move from the Oceania region, into the Asia Football Confederation.

Having qualified for major tournaments by beating the likes of New Zealand, Fiji and Papua New Guinea, the feeling was that if Australia wanted to compete with those teams they would face at a World Cup, they would need a sterner test during qualification.

FIFA ratified the move for Australia to join Asia on 1 July 2005, which would now see them competing against the likes of China, Japan and South Korea.

For Sermanni, who had just been appointed for his second stint as Matildas head coach, the move was crucial to building the foundations of the future success of the team.

'Moving from Oceania into Asia changed the goalposts dramatically. From being in the situation where you had to beat New Zealand to be in the World Cup, you had to go through the Asian Cup to qualify.

'We were viewed as a tough competitor, hard to play against, but in reality, we had never won a game at a World Cup.

'All of a sudden, we have gone into playing in the Asian Cup, where there were three qualifiers and you're playing against North Korea, South Korea, Japan, China and what you'd call the second-tier teams – you had to get to the semi-finals and then win another game just to get to the World Cup.

'We had to re-think what we had to do. We had to go from being a team that was difficult to beat, to a team that won games. And a team that was able to compete in Asia where the type of football is different to what it is in different parts of the world.

'That required a little bit of thinking on how we're going to train, and how we're going to identify players.'

The re-thinking of the game couldn't just be at the top level. With a vast continent and fewer resources than other nations, Sermanni and the Australians were forced to restructure their whole youth pathway and system.

As well as having the youth representative sides within the FFA that Sermanni had been involved with creating during his first spell in charge, football was integrated into the state Institutes of Sport across the country. They were then charged with the responsibility of discovering and developing young players.

Former Matildas Head Coach, Alen Stajcic, who led the side between 2014 and the start of 2019, was one such coach in the new elite pathway. Since the 1970s New South Wales had the proud claim of producing the bulk of the Matildas squad. However, at the time of his appointment there was an NSW drought in the national team.

'When I started at NSWIS [New South Wales Institute of Sport], which is our country's biggest state, we only had one or two players in the Matildas squad, and that seemed a little peculiar that such a strong state, only had one or two representatives,' Stajcic remembered.

A high school sports teacher, Stajcic was now charged with over-seeing the NSWIS women's football programme.

'Coming from a background that had seen me engaged with the youth levels and school levels of football, I worked really hard to try and identify the best players coming through and the various differ-ent forms they were coming through. Some were playing in schools, some were playing in boys teams, some in club teams, and some in programmes under national or state bodies.

'We then tried to put them into a full-time environment. When I started with NSWIS it was a part-time programme, but we very quickly evolved that into a full-time one. We had the likes of Sally Shipard and Leah Blayney, who debuted within almost twelve to eighteen months of the programme going full time, and they were sixteen years old.'

The institute programmes were not just beneficial for the athletes. That the institutes were not just responsible for women's football, but for other sports too, allowed Stajcic to share ideas, best practice, and to come up with plans on how further to develop their young talent with vastly experienced coaches.

This was an opportunity that Stajcic was not going to pass up.

'We [coaches] used to sit together in the same room. It wasn't just NSWIS, it was from other areas too. It was important for our infrastructure and the environments we were working in. The things you learn just by talking is fine, but learning about the level of effort and belief you need to get to that point, I think they are the intangibles you get from mixing and networking with people who have climbed to the top of the world.

'In football we didn't have any role models, we couldn't look to someone who had conquered the world. Australia had been struggling to qualify for men's World Cups, and by the time I had started in 2003, we had never won a game at the Women's World Cup. It was 2007 (in China) when we first won, so we were a fair way behind the pack. Overtaking those elite teams was hard, both on and off the field.'

With a structure in place and regional programmes looking to offer a pathway into the Matildas setup, progress was being made and more players being identified.

Australia went into the 2006 Asian Cup, to be held in Adelaide – their first since moving to the Asian Confederation – with a nine-teen-year-old Sally Shipard, eighteen-year-old goalkeeper, Lydia Williams, and a twenty-year-old Leah Blayney.

Those players, scattered with a squad of experienced heads that included the likes of star striker Sarah Walsh and long-time captain Cheryl Salisbury, were able to make it to the final of the tournament, losing out to China.

That meant qualification for the 2007 World Cup, to be held in China, and an opportunity to try and register the country's first win at FIFA's showpiece event.

Even in reaching the 2006 Asian Cup Final, few were aware of the presence of the Matildas. Departing for the 2007 FIFA Women's World Cup, the Australians quietly slipped out of the country. That was to change in three magical weeks in China.

Coming in with low expectations after failing to win a World Cup match in their previous three attempts, Australia kicked off the tournament with an electric 4-1 win over Ghana. Not only did they beat the African nation, they also held group winners Norway to a 1-1 draw, and knocked Canada out at the group stage by levelling in injury time to draw 2-2.

The quarter-final saw the Matildas take on the powerhouse Brazilians led by the rampaging Marta. Displaying their 'Never Say Die' attitude, Australia pushed the eventual finalists all the way with the Brazilians having to fight hard for their 3-2 victory.

It was a sign that Australia were not just there to make up the numbers, but were now able to compete. Back at home, the Australian public were gaining their first glimpses of the Matildas who were earning praise and pride for their performances and uniquely Australian attitude. This time when they landed on Aussie shores, there was no hiding from the television cameras.

'I think 2006 and 2007 were watershed moments for the team, because it instilled a belief in them that they could win games against top opposition,' said Sermanni.

'That was the platform that started the progress in the programme. We were no longer a team that just went out there and competed. We played the best teams in the world and had confidence to win games.'

While the senior team was thriving and starting to make inroads, Australia's youth teams, or 'Young Matildas' as they are better known, were struggling to adjust to the increased demands of playing in the ultra-competitive Asian Confederation.

Since its launch in 2008, the Under-17s World Cup has been won four times by Asian sides – North Korea twice, South Korea and Japan. In addition, the Under-20 World Cup has been won twice by North Korea and once by Japan. So, Australia was not only trying to qualify for these tournaments, they were having to do it against some of the best teams in the world.

'We didn't have the resource during that period when it came to U-17 and U-20 football,' explained Sermanni.

'We were trying to qualify in difficult environments against some of the best teams. We didn't qualify for anything, but what was important was players had experience of playing against top opposition, in sometimes difficult conditions in countries like Vietnam. We were able to develop players to go into the senior national team with the ability to compete and go and win games.'

Despite the team struggling to qualify for youth World Cups in the region, the benefits of being in the Asian Confederation would soon bear fruit with several Young Matildas gaining invaluable experience.

After the 2007 World Cup, attention turned to the 2010 Asian Cup, which would be held in China.

One of the issues that Australian women's football was facing, was players that were reaching their mid-to-late twenties were retiring from the national team, or football altogether, to pursue other careers. This was fairly common outside of Australia too, with women's football in a number of countries unable to offer the financial security required to make a decent living.

To try and counter this, and to make monitoring players easier and increase competition, a domestic competition in the country was launched in 2008, the W-League, which would allow players to perform between November and February, filling the void left from few to no international fixtures taking place during that period.

This would also allow those aspiring to enter the women's game, an opportunity to make that aspiration a reality, with the FFA reporting an average annual growth rate of 6.3 per cent over the previous five years (2003–2007) of those taking up the sport.[*]

Sermanni explains:

'There were several factors that the W-League was important for. I lobbied because back in those days the international calendar tended to finish about September, so through to January, February, there were no games. We felt we needed something for players to

---

[*] https://www.w-league.com.au/news/westfield-w-league-officially
-launched

play in rather than just turn up at a programme and train for no reason. We also wanted a domestic profile for women's football. We went to the 2007 World Cup and the team captured the attention of the country, so you have that big surge of popularity, but then nothing happens after that and it dies away.

It was also an avenue to develop our younger players and to look at more senior players, plus play week in, week out for three months, so we started the W-League. Put all those factors together, and that system helped those players coming through who were going to the Asia Cup and World Cup.'

The eight-team W-League would become even more important for player development due to the large turnover ahead of the next cycle of tournaments. Between the 2007 World Cup and 2010 Asian Cup, the Matildas lost the likes of captain Cheryl Salisbury, defender Dianne Alagich and midfielder Joanne Peters – three experienced heads who between them had over three decades of national team experience and over three hundred caps.

What that did was open up spots for some of the young players coming through the youth system, which included a fifteen-year-old Sam Kerr, who was playing for Perth Glory in the newly formed league, along with Tameka Butt (Brisbane Roar) and Kyah Simon (Sydney FC).

Another player who was on the radar, but not quite ready for the senior team, was Caitlin Foord. From Shellharbour in New South Wales, Foord was part of Stajcic's NSWIS programme. An exceptional athlete, Foord had been involved in the programme since the age of twelve and was already turning heads.

'The first time I saw her she was twelve years old, playing for a school rep team against seventeen and eighteen-year-old girls, and she had an immediate impact on me,' said Stajcic.

'The way she was taking people on, her tenacity, her skill, her willingness to take people on, was evident right from the start.

'A lot like these other players that I saw at thirteen and fourteen years old, I kept an eye on her and our programme brought players in at fourteen or fifteen, and once they reached that age they came into our full-time environment. By the time Caitlin came in, it was virtually the home training base for the Matildas with a number of senior and youth internationals training with us.'

Around 100 miles up the New South Wales highway, another teenager was creating excitement. With father Gary a former Australian Olympic footballer, Emily van Egmond was born into a football family in Newcastle. With football in her blood, it wasn't long before the intelligent midfielder was on the radar of W-League teams and on the fringes of the national team squad. Meanwhile in Melbourne, Victoria, teenage striker Steph Catley was starting to find her feet in the W-League and beginning to make others take notice.

But like Foord, Van Egmond and Catley would just miss out on a chance to go to China for the 2010 Asian Cup.

While that trio of teens had missed out, Sermanni looked to re-build the Matildas with a cadre of young players with Kerr, Simon and Butt joining Brisbane's Elise Kellond-Knight and Sydney's Teigen Allen in travelling to Chengdu.

As in 2006, the tournament would double up as qualification for the 2011 World Cup. This would be a real test for Australia, who knew that anything less than a semi-final would mean they missed out on a place at the tournament being held in Germany.

The teens weren't there just to make up the numbers. Kellond-Knight and Allen featured in the Australian defence, Butt found space in the midfield and the baby of the team, Kerr, scored her first international goal in Australia's second match in an impressive 3-1 win against South Korea following a 2-0 win over Vietnam.

The final group game saw Australia defeated by China, with the Steel Roses topping the group. The defeat was compounded with the loss of star striker Lisa De Vanna, who suffered a broken leg late in the match. Australia would play its decisive semi-final match against Japan without one of their key weapons.

It was a match that made obvious that the now famous 'Never Say Die' Matildas attitude would be passed down to the next generation. In a match where Japan dominated possession and chances, the Matildas held on before eventually coming out on top by a single Kate Gill goal. For Gill, her goal also fulfilled a promise she had made to her despondent roommate, De Vanna, the night before – that she would take her to the World Cup.

The move into the Asian Confederation was already starting to pay off. In just four years, Australia was set for their second Asian Cup final against North Korea, who had knocked out hosts China in the other semi-final.

Already missing De Vanna and the also injured Butt, monsoon-like conditions would make the task of claiming a first Asian Cup that much harder for Australia.

Kerr would increase her stock by scoring less than twenty minutes into the match, and it looked like that might be enough as the score remained the same as it entered the last twenty minutes, but North Korea would equalise, sending the game into extra-time, and then penalties.

While the teen Kerr had played her part, it would be another teen – Kyah Simon – who would make her mark on Australian football history. Substituted into the game fifteen minutes before the end of normal time, Simon would watch Sally Shipard, Kylie Ledbrook, Kate Gill and Heather Garriock all convert their spot kicks. It was down to eighteen-year-old Simon to win it after North Korea's Yun Son Mi had fired her country's second wide of goalkeeper Melissa Barbieri's post.

A cool and composed Simon stepped up and sent the keeper the wrong way, as Australia claimed their first Asian Cup, with 'We are the Champions' ringing out around the stadium moments after Simon's spot kick had hit the back of the net.

'That was another watershed moment for us,' said Sermanni. Generational transition is not always easy for a team to undertake. By the time the 2010 Asian Cup had come around, Australia had lost almost five hundred matches of experience from the 2007 World Cup squad. The 2010 Asian Cup was set up to be a test of whether the next generation had what it took to build on the work of the veterans.

For Sermanni, gambling on those young players came at a personal cost with success meaning the head coach was sporting newly dyed hair and no moustache due to a bet with his players. But on the pitch, more importantly, the bet on the next generation had already begun to pay off.

'The team took a lot of confidence from that tournament, and when you have young players like Kerr, Simon, Clare Polkinghorne and Elise Kellond-Knight all starting to make a name for themselves, it prepared them well for what was to come the following year at the World Cup.'

So Australia was going to the World Cup, and they would have just over a year to prepare for the tournament, which was due to kick-off in June 2011.

By the time preparation for Germany 2011 came around, Sermanni was a World Cup veteran. The head coach had led the team in Sweden 1995 and China 2007 and with that came invaluable knowledge.

The priority now for Sermanni was to ensure he identified the most efficient approach to prepare his squad for that tournament, but also to identify who would be part of it.

Kellond-Knight, Kerr and Simon had shone at the Asian Cup and were pushing for starting places within Sermanni's senior squad, while Foord and Van Egmond were impressing in the Matildas youth setup.

Drawing on his experience from previous campaigns, Sermanni decided to defy conventional wisdom. Instead of arranging a whole host of international friendlies in the lead up to the World Cup, he decided to get the players together every three to four weeks for training camps. This would allow him not only to look at a number of players, but also to actually have his players gelling and learning to work with each other.

'The traditional plan was you play as many internationals as you can leading into a World Cup. But because we had such a potential turnover in the squad, what we decided to do was basically scrap looking at travelling to play internationals. The problem you have when you are looking for games, you have to travel, because teams rarely come to Australia.

'You just don't get enough training time with the players. You take eighteen to twenty players, and six or seven of them won't get much game time. So we got the team together for three to four days every three to four weeks. That gave us a chance to have a bigger number of players, and a squad where players could get to know each other.'

Amongst those players brought in were Foord and Van Egmond, who joined fellow teenagers in Simon, Kerr and Allen. All five players had performed incredibly well in the previous W-League season to continue to force their way into the forefront of Sermanni's mind. However, Foord, who had burst onto the W-League scene that season, had yet to taste the full national team environment or be tested at the international level.

Australia would play two friendlies just before the World Cup commenced, against New Zealand, with one of the games behind closed doors.

Foord would make her debut in the first of the two games, and would score within ten minutes.

'I actually remember very clearly the game,' said Foord. 'It was Heather Garriock's hundredth cap and she was presented with this really nice trophy with all her games and where she had scored. I just recall looking at that and being like "that's really cool". This was my first cap and I wanted to be like that as well.

'After that I remember walking out, and I scored as well. To have my mum and family in the crowd was pretty special too.'

Australia would go on to win that game 3-0 with a team that also started with Kerr and Van Egmond, with fellow youngsters Kellond-Knight and Butt on the bench.

The one thing Sermanni was not afraid to do was to throw youngsters in at the deep end. Foord's fast-track through to the senior team highlighted the positive work being done in the Matildas youth programme and within the regional institutes. But what it also highlighted, was that the Australian mentality was fearless, and that naivety and inexperience can work in your favour.

'Aussies don't really give a bollox,' according to Sermanni. 'A fifteen-year-old kid like Sam Kerr, Emily van Egmond or Caitlin Foord walk into a national team camp and are never overawed. That's an Aussie thing, "I'm here, let's go."'

Change was certainly in the air and with it came some uncertainty for some senior players.

For De Vanna, walking back in was truly a culture shock. She was the undisputed superstar of the team and had spent time away from the squad playing alongside Abby Wambach, Sonia Bompastor and Homare Sawa for Washington Freedom/MagicJack in the USA's Women's Professional Soccer (WPS) league.

In that fully professional environment the striker thrived, feeling challenged, empowered by and learning from legends of the game she admired. Returning to Australia, De Vanna, who was the one-time wunderkind of Australian football who grew up looking up to the likes of the retired Salisbury, Alicia Ferguson, Dianne Alagich and Joanne Peters, was now a veteran of the team at just twenty-six.

She admits the transition to the new surroundings was tough; not because she didn't like the players around her, but put simply, the new dynamic was so different.

'When you get into a national team with big personalities and legends of the game, you look up to them,' remembered De Vanna.

'Then one day, as still a young player, you become one of them, a senior player. That was a big turning point in 2011. The team was very inexperienced and you wouldn't think that a few years down the line these young players would become superstars for Australia.'

Sermanni saw his key player's struggles but had to let the situation play out.

'The squad had started to change and Lisa had been away for several months, and then came in for the games with New Zealand in May 2011,' he remembered.

'She arrived into the squad, walked into the team room, and the team she had left was significantly changed to the team she had walked into.

'That really freaked Lisa out a little, she was surrounded by a load of young players who she knew, but didn't know. She found that difficult to deal with because she thought that "we have all these players, and I don't know how good they are. How are we going to cope, how are we going to get results?"

'She found it hard to cope with the change. It was a critical time, and from a coaching perspective, it was a case of "you need to change and deal with this, or it's not going to work".'

After a number of small conflicts, Sermanni was forced to suspend De Vanna from the team, asking her to leave the camp during the friendlies with New Zealand just a month before the World Cup was due to start.

The suspension was never intended to be long term, with coach

Sermanni always planning to bring her back ahead of the trip to Germany.

'The key thing from my perspective, is it was always my intention to bring her back and take her to the World Cup. We needed everyone on board, everyone confident and everyone on the same page. Lisa had a rethink, so we brought her back in for the World Cup.'

Having everyone on the same page would result in an Australian squad for Germany 2011 that would include six teenagers – Simon, Foord, Van Egmond, Kerr, Allen and goalkeeper Casey Dumont – and three twenty-year-olds in Kellond-Knight, Butt and Ellyse Perry, meaning a squad with an average age of just under twenty-two; the youngest squad Australia had ever sent to a World Cup.

The squad would include thirteen World Cup debutantes in total, and for those players, the news that a lifelong dream was in reach was unforgettable.

'That was a really special occasion,' remembered Kellond-Knight. 'Tom did it individually. He took us into a room, sat us down and just said "you're coming".

'I thought that was pretty simple and pretty easy, so there was nothing else to really say about it. He said you're part of the team and I hope you're ready to come with us.'

At just sixteen, Foord would find out about her place in the squad thanks to a call while in the car with her mum, Simone.

It was fitting that the teen would find out the news with her biggest supporter at her side as she had been her whole life. A single mother, Simone Foord had sacrificed plenty to give her prodigiously talented daughter every chance to reach her dreams, often driving four hours a day to take Foord to and from training sessions, as well as working multiple jobs to afford her fees and equipment.

After putting the phone down to tell her mum of her news, Foord was in for a surprise of her own – and not a welcome one.

'She knew already!' she laughed. 'Mum was excited as well, but I was annoyed she knew before me.'

The announcement of the squad came three weeks before Australia's first game of the tournament against 2007 World Cup finalists Brazil. While Australia was going to the World Cup full of confidence after two tune-up matches against New Zealand, the opening match in Mönchengladbach would demonstrate whether Sermanni's changes to the preparation would pay dividends.

Led by then five-time FIFA World Player of the Year and 2007 Golden Ball and Golden Boot winner Marta, Brazil were a hugely gifted side with match winners across the park like Formiga and Cristiane.

Despite the Brazilians' obvious football pedigree, the Australians would not be fazed. There is an adage in football that states 'if you are good enough, you are old enough'. Sermanni subscribed to that adage and put his faith in his young team, starting five of his players aged twenty and under with Foord given her first competitive start at right-back. This would mean coming up against the fleet-footed Marta. In Foord's case, youth was an advantage on many levels.

'I remember standing in the tunnel and obviously the changing room before,' said Foord of the moment she would make her World Cup debut.

'A number of the girls had been there before, so they knew what they were getting into. I could sense the nervousness and you could almost say fear because it was such a big game. I just remember being fine. I was young and didn't really know so I was like "why is everyone so scared?"

'I guess I was so young and was just soaking it all in, it didn't really affect me that much. Walking out, I just remember thinking this is the coolest thing ever, walking out and seeing these crowds that were actually here to see me play.

'I think even now, when there are a lot of people watching you, you almost want to show off and show how good you are. I just remember thinking, "I'm going to go and play the best I can and be the best player I can be." I was just really excited.'

Australia's youngsters stood up well to the challenge of Brazil, with Foord particularly impressive in nullifying the threat of Marta, showing no signs of being overawed by the challenge and making an early impression on the tournament. However, it would be a fifty-fourth-minute goal from Brazilian defender Rosana that separated the two sides and condemned Australia to an opening-game defeat.

The defeat hurt the Australians, who had showed no signs of inferiority or being intimidated by Brazil. But with the close proximity of matches in a World Cup, they had no time to dwell on the result, and would have to lick their wounds and prepare for a match with the unpredictable Equatorial Guinea, and star forward, Genoveva Añonma.

Foord would miss out on that match, but fellow teenager Kerr was unleashed on the African nation in Bochum, while Van Egmond and Kellond-Knight kept their place in the starting XI.

Australia started the brighter, controlling possession in the early exchanges, but would go into half-time level after a Leena Khamis goal early on was cancelled out by Añonma after an unfortunate error from defender, Servet Uzunlar.

The leveller, however, came after one of the most bizarre moments of the whole tournament, when Australia were denied a clear penalty after the most unusual piece of defending from Equatorial Guinea's Bruna.

Khamis found some space in the box after a Garriock cross, and from close range she sliced an effort onto the post. The ball rebounded back to Bruna, but instead of hacking it away, the Equatorial Guinea defender grabbed the ball with both hands. Realising her mistake, she simply dropped it to the floor, but no penalty was awarded. It certainly goes down as one of the oddest moments of a Women's World Cup and for those few seconds, it was as if time had stood still.

But Australia shook off that moment of madness and started the second half much like the first, and would retake the lead thanks to one of their emerging teenagers. Khamis latched onto a ball down the left-hand side, before crossing for Van Egmond, who smashed the ball home with a fierce right-footed effort from just inside the box – a finish that any striker would have been proud of.

It was her first goal for her country, and she had scored it at a World Cup. It was a moment to remember for the seventeen-year-old who became one of the youngest players ever to score at FIFA's showpiece competition – just nine days before her eighteenth birthday. The kids were demonstrating that they were alright.

De Vanna then added a third to all but kill the match, but there was one late scare for Australia to make it a nervy last period of the match. While Van Egmond was experiencing the euphoria of having scored her first goal for her country at a World Cup, her teammate Uzunlar was at the opposite end of the spectrum after a second mistake. Again, she was caught in possession by Añonma, who slotted home to make it 3-2.

It didn't matter; Australia had earned their second ever World Cup win and knew that a win against Norway would see them advance to the quarter-finals. The Scandinavians had looked unconvincing in their opening two matches, defeating Equatorial Guinea by a solitary Emile Haavi goal, before crashing to a 3-0 defeat to Brazil. Australia's young guns had every chance.

That game with the Norwegians, who had been a force in the early years of the World Cup but were going through somewhat of a lean spell, would take place in Leverkusen, and Sermanni would rotate his players once again, bringing Foord back into the starting line-up, and dropping Van Egmond to the bench. But in starting seventeen-year-old Kerr and a now twenty-year-old Simon up front, it showed the faith the Scottish coach had in his squad, in what was one of Australia's most important matches in their history.

The first half saw a tense forty-five minutes with nothing to separate the two teams, but it was Norway that would break the deadlock eleven minutes after half time, and it was again a defensive mix up that was taken advantage of.

A harmless ball played over the top of the defence was not dealt with by Foord or keeper Melissa Barbieri, and striker Elise Thorsnes nipped in to poke the ball past the stranded goalkeeper, before blasting it into an empty net. Disaster for Australia, who were now just over half an hour from going home.

But the fearless 'not giving a bollox' approach that Sermanni talked about, was evident from his players less than a minute after going behind. De Vanna was able to find some space down the Australian left-hand side, before playing a cross into the box for Kyah Simon.

Just over twelve months before, Simon had made history for Australia with the Aboriginal flag hanging over the stadium balustrades at the Asia Cup. She would make another annotation in the Australian football story.

When the young striker opened up her body and side-footed a shot into the bottom corner to bring her country level, she became the first indigenous Australian to score at a World Cup. Another goal for Australia, another youngster who had earned it.

That wasn't enough for Simon, as with four minutes remaining, with both teams pushing for a winner, she met a Kim Carroll cross to head home and send her country through.

'We earned it,' said Sermanni. 'There were some nervous moments, but we showed a fearless attitude and deserved to go through.'

Australia had played three group matches, and all five teenagers named to the squad on 8 June had played some part in their progression to the knockout stage.

The key to that progression, according to midfielder Kellond-Knight, who played every minute during the group stages, was trust.

'There was a lot of freedom, that's Tom's style. He lets you show your personality on and off the field, and I like that. He doesn't really have reins on you, and I think you get the best out of players when that happens.'

The Matildas' road to the semi-final was blocked by Sweden, who had topped a group that included the United States after beating them in their first-round encounter.

It would be a big ask for Sermanni's side, with the head coach making more changes from the side that beat Norway, which included bringing in twenty-year-old defender Ellyse Perry who had played a total of one minute during the group stages.

Perry had already won a World Cup for Australia, but with a bat and ball in hand, rather than a ball at her feet. The New South Wales born player was competing in both football and cricket for her country at the time, and was the Player of the Match in the final of the T20 Women's World Cup Final in the West Indies, the shortest form of international cricket, as her country triumphed over New Zealand.

So big matches and big occasions were nothing new to Perry, who lined up against a strong Sweden side in Augsburg with a semi-final at stake.

It would prove to be a game too far, with Sweden's Therese Sjogran and Lisa Dahlkvist putting Australia's opponents 2-0 up inside sixteen minutes. Dahlkvist's goal was a simple header due to a lack of marking in the box.

Australia would have it all to do in the second half, and they were given a lifeline from their World Cup winner, who lit up the match with one of the goals of the tournament.

A short corner was played to Perry on the edge of the box, and with the Swedes slow to vacate their area, she clipped a left-foot shot past Hedvig Lindahl in the Sweden goal, into the top-corner. It was a moment of brilliance from Perry, who will have been more used to lofting cricket balls over the boundary for six, than finding the top corner of the net from her usual defensive position.

But as her side went in search of an equaliser, yet another defensive lapse would put the game out of reach, when a short back pass to keeper Barbieri was intercepted by Sweden's star striker, Lotta Schelin. It was a simple task for Schelin, as she prodded the ball past the onrushing Australia keeper, before side-footing into an empty net.

Schelin, one of the game's greats who retired in 2018 due to health concerns, was the last player Australia would have wanted to present the ball to.

That was the killer goal, and Australia were heading home after a second consecutive World Cup quarter-final that had been lit up by their young squad.

'When I look back on it now, in hindsight, I'd have done things differently against Sweden,' said Sermanni. 'I don't like to look back too much because we had an amazing tournament, but I'd have done a few things different.'

Despite the exit, Australia had matched their best performance at a World Cup, and they had done it with a squad of players that had an average age of under twenty-two.

Seven teenagers had appeared for the side over the course of the tournament, and they had helped to bring Australia's first win over a European nation at a World Cup, while causing considerable anxiety for a Brazil side that went on to lose the most dramatic of quarter-finals to the United States on penalties.

There was also individual recognition for the Matildas, with defender Kellond-Knight named in the FIFA All Star team.

With the team already back in Australia when the news was announced, Kellond-Knight had not even been notified of her inclusion, and found out while out with a friend.

'That was a shock, there was no way I expected to be named in the All-Star team. It was after the World Cup I remember, and nobody had even told me. A friend said to me while we were on holiday, "Hey, I think I just read a tweet that you're in the World Cup All-Star team," and I was like, "You've got to be kidding." It just never occurred that it would happen, it was never on my radar.'

For Foord, inclusion in the team for the World Cup was huge recognition, considering she was making her tournament debut as a sixteen-year-old. But she would go on to receive even more praise in winning an award that would make the world of women's football stand up and notice. Along with being named in the All-Star team, she was also awarded the Young Player of the Tournament.

'That was honestly just a massive surprise, and at the time I didn't really know what I had won, I didn't even know that trophy existed,' she said. 'That was the first year it came into the World Cup. I only had Facebook back then and I remember my page being pretty active. I was actually travelling after the World Cup, so I wasn't actually there. Not until now that I look back at it do I appreciate it, and I am really proud of the tournament that I had.'

Foord and Kellond-Knight were part of a team that mixed both youth and experience, with that blend seeing the side progress as far as they ever had done, giving major nations like Brazil, Norway and Sweden a run for their money.

But it's what has happened since that really highlights just how special the young crop of players that Sermanni put his faith in were, and are, as Australian women's football goes from strength to strength.

In 2011, Foord was named the Asian Confederation's Young

Player of the Year and in 2016, was named Women's Footballer of the Year, becoming only the third Australian to be awarded the accolade. Her teammate, Sam Kerr, then followed that up by winning the same award in 2017.

While Kerr had a relatively quiet World Cup in 2011 compared with some of her fellow youngsters, it is she that has gone on to become one of the world's most recognised players, winning award after award in her home country, as well as becoming a household name in America's National Women's Soccer League.

The name 'Kerr' is blazoned on the shirts of many Australian women's football fans young and old, with the East Fremantle-born striker becoming one of the country's top athletes – male or female.

While Kerr takes many of the headlines, Kellond-Knight has quietly become one of the cornerstones of the Australian team. In 2015 she was named in the FIFA All Star team once again.

In 2018, Kellond-Knight became just the seventh Australian to pass one hundred caps for her country when she captained the side against England in October 2018, describing it as 'an honour', as she continues to be recognised as one of the best defensive midfielders in the game. She, Emily van Egmond and Tameka Butt, have been key components of the Australia midfield since the 2011 tournament, and much like Kerr, Foord and Simon, were all part of the 2015 World Cup in Canada, where again, Australia – under the leadership of Alen Stajcic – would reach a quarter-final before succumbing to Brazil.

Stajcic, who nurtured many of Australia's young talents during his time at NSWIS, took over the head coach role of the Matildas in 2014 from Dutch coach Hesterine de Reus, who had replaced Sermanni at the end of 2012.

Under Stajcic's leadership, Australia joined the elite of global women's football, selling out stadiums across the country and not just competing with the best nations in the world, but beating them.

Eight years later, Australian stars in their prime are those who gained invaluable experience at that 2011 World Cup. But they will be progressing under a new coach, after Stajcic lost his job with the team in January 2019.

Before his departure, he said: 'I think all the players have catapulted this team into the mainstream of Aussie sport.

'It's gone to a place people probably wouldn't have imagined two or three years ago, let alone ten years ago, when women's football was barely a blip on the radar.

'Sam Kerr is such a leading light, she has been elevated above the pack in terms of her media profile, but even in 2016 it was Caitlin Foord named Asia player of the year, so it's all pretty new. We are now winning awards in front of Australian Rules Football (AFL), Rugby and even men's sport. Our team has been elevated to that level of winning awards in terms of popularity and reach in front of those teams.

'But we know there is so much more work to be done. Even though we have come a long way, we have a lot of work to do to sustain that interest and level.'

Lifting up a Nation
from Tragedy

....

'Nadeshiko, the world number ones!' read a headline in the *Asahi Shimbun* after one of Japan's greatest sporting triumphs, and the greatest achieved by any Asian football team – male or female.[*]

But Japan's victory at the 2011 Women's World Cup in Germany meant so much more than just a trophy and medal around a player's neck.

When they defeated overwhelming favourites the United States in Frankfurt in front of a crowd of over forty-eight thousand fans, they didn't just win for those who followed the team. They didn't just win for those who followed football back home. No, they had won the tournament for 127 million Japanese people who just four months earlier had seen their country crippled by one of the most devastating tragedies the country had ever experienced.

When captain Homare Sawa lofted the trophy above her head, it was for a nation. A nation crying tears of joy, when four months earlier, it was tears of desolation.

This is their story.

To qualify for the 2011 World Cup in Germany, Japan would have to finish as one of the top three nations at the Asia Cup, which was held at the Chengdu Sports Centre in China in May 2010.

[*] https://www.theguardian.com/world/2011/jul/18/japan-womens-world-cup-reaction-joy

Having been disappointingly knocked out of the 2007 World Cup at the group stage, ironically in China, Japan knew that 2011 was an opportunity to right some wrongs.

With one of the game's most gifted forwards in Homare Sawa, who had already played in four World Cups, Japan had a genuine game-changer who could create something out of nothing. Alongside midfielder Aya Miyama, who like Sawa had played professionally in the United States and was something of a dead-ball specialist, Japan had two players who were admired the world over, but had never been able to succeed on the world stage.

The Asia Cup in China was no foregone conclusion for the Japanese and they would need to be at their best to qualify for another World Cup. With Australia having moved over to the Asian Confederation in 2007 from Oceania, it made for a competitive qualification with North Korea, South Korea and hosts China all capable of claiming a World Cup spot.

Head Coach Norio Sasaki's side were drawn with North Korea, Thailand and Myanmar in their Asia Cup group and would need to finish in the top two to qualify for the semi-finals. With China, South Korea and Australia in the other group, Japan had been dealt a kind hand, and looked overwhelming favourites to top the group.

And top the group they did – it was a comfortable passage to the last four.

The Japanese opened with an 8-0 win over Myanmar, before beating Thailand 4-0 and North Korea 2-1. Three wins out of three, and their reward was a semi-final against Australia.

The Australians had been making steady progress under Head Coach Tom Sermanni, and had a good crop of young players starting to make a name for themselves (see the chapter on Australia's Golden Generation).

Despite that group of young players starting to impose themselves on the Australian team, it was the experience of striker Kate

Gill that would prove decisive, as she scored the only goal of the game to hand Australia the win over Japan, confining them to the third place play-off that they'd have to win to confirm their place at the following year's World Cup.

That match would be against China, who had been beaten by North Korea in their semi-final. It was unthinkable that one of these sides would miss out on a World Cup spot, but with Australia and the North Koreans already confirming their places, one of the Asia heavyweights would be staying at home.

Forwards Kozue Ando and Sawa would prove the difference for Japan as they ran out 2-0 winners over China to book their place alongside Australia and North Korea, meaning the 1999 finalists would have to miss out.

Japan had qualified for every World Cup since its inception in 1991, so it was inconceivable for such a talented group of players not to continue that run and try and end Asia's search for a first senior World Cup, with the men having never tasted victory either.

Coach Sasaki would have a year to prepare his team for Germany with the Asia Cup completed thirteen months before the big kick-off in Berlin.

When the draw took place, Japan would find themselves paired with New Zealand, Mexico and England, and would open the tournament against the Football Ferns in Bochum.

They had faced England at the 2007 World Cup in China, and despite securing a late draw thanks to an Aya Miyama free-kick with virtually the last kick of the game, they were unable to progress to the knockout stages after a defeat to Germany.

As preparation for the 2011 event, Japan would warm up for their sixth World Cup by travelling to Portugal to take part in the annual Algarve Cup for the very first time.

While deemed a friendly competition, the tournament, which has been running since 1994, is well known for attracting some of the best teams in the world, with the United States, Sweden and Norway amongst the sides who also travelled to the Portuguese south coast.

The tournament takes place every year at the end of February into the beginning of March, and Head Coach Sasaki took a strong squad to ensure players likely to go to the World Cup would get vital minutes.

Wins against Norway and Finland were only soured by a narrow defeat to the United States, which meant Japan finished second in their group of four, and would play Sweden for a third-place finish.

Goals from Megumi Kamionobe and Nahomi Kawasumi would be enough as they defeated the Swedes by two goals to one to finish behind the US and Iceland.

That game against Sweden, on 9 March 2011, would come just two days before one of the most devastating tragedies of this millennium.

On 11 March 2011, just three months before Japan were due to kick-off their World Cup campaign in Bochum, the country was hit by an earthquake, that was recorded as magnitude nine, around 45 miles off the northeast shore and about 250 miles from Tokyo.

That earthquake would create the most devastating tsunami, lifting the seafloor over 30 feet over an area the size of Connecticut, creating waves of around 100 feet, flooding an estimated area of approximately 217 square miles.*

In some areas, waves travelled up to six miles inland, destroying all before them – homes, buildings, cars, swiping up anything in their path and carrying debris in scenes many will have never

* https://www.livescience.com/39110-japan-2011-earthquake-tsunami-facts.html

witnessed before. The tsunami also caused damage to the Fukushima Daiichi Nuclear Power Plant, which resulted in a nuclear meltdown and release of radioactive materials. That nuclear disaster would be particularly significant for two of Japan's World Cup squad members – defender Aya Sameshima and forward Karina Maruyama – who both worked at the plant before the tsunami and had friends still working there.*

Almost twenty thousand people died as a result of the disaster, with hundreds of thousands more left homeless as many homes were destroyed. It was the fifth largest earthquake ever recorded.

All of a sudden, football seemed insignificant. The Japan women's team would be going to a World Cup knowing that so many of their people had suffered the most traumatic episode.

While there was little they could do to help those affected, sport often unites a country at the most difficult of times, and Japan now had an opportunity to bring attention to their country by being successful at a global tournament.

Defender Saki Kumagai, who was just twenty-one going into the World Cup, explained that while her teammates were shocked by the scenes they saw unfold, they tried to remain professional as they entered the World Cup just weeks after the tragedy.

'It was utterly shocking,' she said.

'I couldn't believe my eyes when I saw tsunami footage from Japan on TV. We all were just focusing on doing our best as professional footballers as that was the only thing we could do back then, and strongly hoped our performance encouraged people in Japan. Also, after each game we heard the message, "Thank you, you made us feel hopeful" from the affected area. It helped us massively to concentrate on the tournament.'

* https://www.independent.co.uk/hei-fi/entertainment/japans-joy-from-nuclear-disaster-to-world-cup-triumph-2316150.html

Japan opened their World Cup campaign with an unconvincing 2-1 win over New Zealand thanks to goals from Yuki Nagasato and Aya Miyama, before heading to Leverkusen and disposing of Mexico 4-0 – Homare Sawa netting a wonderful hat-trick.

Their final group game would come against England, with a win or draw cementing a first-place position in the group and a potentially more straightforward quarter-final against a group runner-up.

A crowd of over twenty thousand showed up in the Augsburg sunshine to watch the two group favourites battle it out, but it was Hope Powell's England that would spring a surprise and overcome a below-par Japan.

Goals from striker Ellen White and winger Rachel Yankey saw off a Japanese side that struggled to impose themselves on the match and fail to beat England for a second World Cup in succession. The defeat meant they had qualified, but had finished second, and they would now have to face the world champions and hosts, Germany.

'It was deeply disappointing,' said Kumagai.

'We wanted to be finishing first. Having said that, the loss to England gave us a chance to reflect upon ourselves and prepare to do well for the rest of the tournament.'

Their quarter-final match with Germany would involve travelling to Wolfsburg and would see forwards Yuki Nagasato and Kozue Ando potentially come up against some of their club teammates.

Germany's Frauen-Bundesliga was seen as a desirable destination for overseas players with clubs, especially at the top, offering more professional environments. They were also successful, with German sides often reaching the latter stages of the UEFA Women's Champions League. Nagasato actually won Europe's premier competition just a year earlier with her club Turbine Potsdam, scoring in a penalty shoot-out win over Lyon in the final. For her, and for Ando, who played for Duisburg, the game against Germany would be extra special.

Playing in front of the host nation's supporters would see Japan have to overcome a partisan crowd as well as early German pressure, with the world champions looking to take control from the off. Forward Celia Okoyino da Mbabi and midfielder Melanie Behringer both went close in the first half, with Sasaki's side struggling to impose themselves in front of the twenty-six thousand strong crowd. They did start to pose more of a threat in the second forty-five minutes, with Aya Miyama seeing two efforts fly over the crossbar, while defensively they were containing the German front line a lot better.

Neither side could find the vital winner during ninety minutes, which meant extra-time.

According to journalist David McNeil, writing for *The Independent*, Japan coach Sasaki had sat the players down before the Germany game and showed them video images of post-meltdown Fukushima, 'a strategy designed to motivate the team's players'.*

As already mentioned, Karina Maruyama was one of two players in the squad who worked at the plant, and that move by Sasaki clearly had its desired effect, as it would be she who would become the hero.

Three minutes into the second period of extra-time, Sawa picked up the ball just beyond the halfway line and clipped a beautifully weighted pass beyond the Germany defence. Maruyama latched onto the pass, and from a tight angle, riffled the ball past Nadine Angerer in the Germany goal into the bottom left-hand corner to give Japan the lead and silence the home crowd.

Wild celebrations followed, but they would still have to sustain twelve minutes of late pressure from the home side as the crowd became more and more anxious.

* https://www.independent.co.uk/hei-fi/entertainment/japans-joy-from-nuclear-disaster-to-world-cup-triumph-2316150.html

But the hosts could not find a way through, and the world and European champions, were out.

Japan had progressed to the semi-final of a World Cup for the first time, and they had done it against the odds, against a side that hadn't lost a game at FIFA's showpiece tournament since 1999.

Duisburg forward Ando had double reason to celebrate, as the victory would take place on her birthday, as she outlined in an interview with FIFA World Museum in 2016. 'When I think of the World Cup in 2011, I have to mention the quarter-final against Germany. It was a special one for me as I felt Germany was my second home after transferring to the Bundesliga in 2010.

'Playing against my teammates as opponents and with the "away" end packed with German supporters, and coincidentally it was my birthday ... I had so many feelings and worked hard to show my best on the pitch."*

Japan were one game from a final, and it would be Sweden who would be looking to spoil the party as the two teams met in Frankfurt, knowing that the winner would be playing the United States, who had beaten France 3-1 earlier that evening.

Sweden were dealt a blow in the warmup before the match, when captain Caroline Seger was forced to withdraw from the starting line-up after aggravating a calf injury. Sweden's enforcer would be missing in the middle of the park, which would no doubt give Japan more space and time on the ball.

The key to any big match is to ensure you don't go behind early and make the task even more difficult. Sadly for Japan, it only took Sweden ten minutes to open the scoring, and it came as a result of an uncharacteristic mistake from, of all people, Sawa.

* http://www.fifamuseum.com/stories/blog/kozue-ando-on-winning-asia-s-first-world-cup-title-2616906/

The Japan number ten played a square pass that was intercepted by Josefine Oqvist, who ran at the Japanese defence and fired a deflected shot past goalkeeper Ayumi Kaihori. It was a disastrous start for Japan, but there was still plenty of time for them to claw the game back.

It only took them nine minutes to level in what was one of the more unorthodox goals you are likely to see. Miyama found some space down Japan's left and fired a cross into the box. Forward Nahomi Kawasumi threw her head at the ball, missed it, but the ball hit her right leg and went through the legs of Sweden keeper Hedvig Lindahl. Not one you can practise in training, but Japan didn't care; they were level going into half-time.

The second-half started at a frenetic pace and Japan almost took the lead when midfielder Shinobu Ohno's dipping half-volley clipped the top of the crossbar from fully 25-yards – it would have been a contender for goal of the tournament.

Following good build-up play down the right on the hour mark, Japan would take the lead after the ball was swung into the box. Lindahl came to claim it but her punch was ineffective. Sawa was on hand to head into an empty net for her fourth goal of the tournament.

Japan were now in control, and they would kill the game off four minutes after Sawa's header. It was Kawasumi again on target, with a moment of brilliant improvisation.

Lindahl came out to deal with a long ball which was meant for Ando, but her clearance fell straight to Kawasumi, who hit a looping shot from 35 yards. The effort flew over a stranded Lindahl and bounced into the back of the net. A finish worthy of winning any match, and win the match it did. Sweden were unable to find a way back into the match, and for the first time in their history, Japan would be going to a World Cup Final, the first for an Asian side since China lost to the United States in 1999.

It was a moment to cherish for Japan, who twenty years earlier at the inaugural World Cup in 1991, had lost 8-0 to the same opponents.

Football in Japan had come a long way.

Perhaps it was fate. Perhaps a lucky omen. But Japan wouldn't have to travel for the final of the World Cup, as it was to be held at the very stadium in which they had beaten Sweden, the Commerzbank Arena in Frankfurt.

They would need fate and the lucky omens to overcome the United States, a nation they had not beaten in twenty-five previous attempts, with twenty-two defeats and three draws.

Young defender Kumagai, who would have the responsibility of trying to stop one of the most potent strikers in the tournament, Abby Wambach, was under no illusions as to how difficult the task would be.

'Just before the World Cup we'd lost twice against USA, also we'd never beaten them before. We were aware how powerful they were and it was obvious that the final would be a really tough match for us.'

The one advantage for Japan was they had nothing to lose. They were huge underdogs having never been to a final, and with their record against the US being so poor, few gave them a chance.

On the flip side, the US had the weight of a nation on their shoulders. When Brandi Chastain scored the winning penalty for the United States in the final against China in 1999, it was supposed to be the start of a long period of dominance for America. But in both 2003 and 2007, they had failed to make the final, and continuing talk of 'the 99ers' was not going to go away until they lifted another World Cup.

While the crowd had a strongly American flavour, for the Japanese team, they knew their biggest supporters were more than 5,000 miles away.

'They touched us deep in our souls,' Aya Miyama told reporters following their victory against Sweden.

'We could feel the energy coming from everyone back in Japan watching on TV,' concurred Sasaki in a television interview prior to the final. 'I'm stunned.'*

Japan and the US were known for having different styles, with the Asians keen on possession, and the Americans more used to quick transition, and with those different approaches, the forty-eight thousand spectators were treated to the most entertaining and tense World Cup Final since the tournament began.

Japan knew they were in for a long night when midfielder Lauren Cheney almost opened the scoring for the US after twenty-five seconds, but her effort was saved by Kaihori, much to the relief of her teammates.

Being quicker and more physical, USA dominated the early proceedings, pressing Japan to ensure they were unable to keep the ball and settle into the game. Cheney, Carli Lloyd and Megan Rapinoe all went close for the United States, before Wambach rattled the crossbar with a rasping drive on twenty-nine minutes. A let-off for Japan, and they needed to find a way to stop the onslaught.

Shots from both sides continued to fly after the half-time interval, and it would take until the sixty-ninth minute for the deadlock to be broken, and it would come from substitute Alex Morgan – a twenty-one-year-old who was seen as one of the US's brightest young stars.

She latched onto a through ball from Rapinoe, showed her strength to hold off a defender, and lashed the ball past Kaihori. It was no more than USA deserved, and now Japan had it all to do.

* https://www.huffingtonpost.com/santiago-halty/a-cup-half-full-the-socia_b_6480932.html

But Japan had shown throughout the tournament that heart and persistence can go a long way. They had fought back from a goal behind against Sweden, and they had knocked out the hosts and world champions, Germany. Twelve minutes after Morgan's opener, that heart was on display yet again, as they levelled. A cross into the box from the right-hand side caused confusion amongst defenders Ali Krieger and Rachel Buhler. The ball ping-ponged in the area and Aya Miyama was there to poke home past Hope Solo to level for Japan. A nation at home was watching, and again, they had been given something to smile about.

Japan would have to endure extra-time for the second time in three matches as the match finished 1-1.

The Frankfurt crowd had been provided a real treat, and they were about to get thirty minutes more of high tempo, end-to-end football.

The first half of extra-time would continue much the same with both sides seeking out a winner, until a minute before half-time when the US restored their lead.

Rapinoe saw a cross blocked with the ball deflecting to Morgan. She took two touches before crossing for Wambach, who benefited from an error from Kumagai to head home and become the USA's all-time leading scorer at World Cups.

Japan would have fifteen second-half minutes to rescue their World Cup hopes – surely they couldn't come back again against a side that still looked strong and were still capable of adding another goal?

Many who followed Japan's story from the devastating tsunami on 11 March, to the final they had overcome the odds to reach on 17 July, felt it was meant to be for Norio Sasaki's team. They may have had a point.

Captain Sawa had been the anchor point for Nadeshiko through-out the tournament, her calmness and leadership guiding the team to heights unknown.

'If you're having a tough time, watch my back,' Sawa had told her teammates in the pre-match rallying cry. 'I will be there, playing with everything I've got to lead you.'*

Three minutes before the USA were about to be crowned world champions, Japan's shining light, playing in her fifth World Cup, would score to take the match to penalties.

A corner whipped in from the left-hand side saw Sawa meet the ball with the most audacious of volleys, that took a slight deflection and flew past Solo in the US goal. It was one of the goals of the tournament, and one of the moments of the tournament. Japan just did not know when they were defeated, and as the game went into a shootout, the feeling was that for the first time in the contest, the pendulum had swung in their favour.

With the match kicking-off at 3.45am Tokyo time, 10.4 million (peaking at fifteen million) TV viewers in Japan, would have to wait a little longer before they could grab their breakfast.

That pendulum swing in favour of Japan would see the USA completely capitulate from the penalty spot.

Kaihori saved from midfielder Shannon Boxx, diving down to her left. 0-0

Miyama then coolly stepped up and left Solo stranded. 0-1

Carli Lloyd then blasted her effort over the bar. 0-1

Solo saved from Nagasato, diving down to her right. 0-1

Kaihori saved from Tobin Heath, diving down to her right. 0-1

Sakaguchi slotted underneath the diving Solo to score. 0-2

Wambach blasted her spot-kick high into the net to score the USA's first. 1-2

With Japan 2-1 up and ready to take their fourth spot-kick, it was left to their twenty-one-year-old defender, Kumagai, to bring glory to Japan and Asia.

---

* http://olympics.time.com/2012/07/19/womens-football-nadeshiko-japan-homare-sawa/

'Luckily, our goalkeeper had already saved some penalty kicks before my turn, so I didn't feel too nervous as there would still be the next chance even if I missed. I was just concentrating to kick my utmost.'

Kumagai placed the ball, and took a number of steps back, with her focus very much on the goal, and not the ball. Goalkeeper Solo was stood a few yards off her line, swinging her arms in an attempt to make the goal look smaller, and her presence more prominent.

It didn't work.

The young defender jogged up to the ball and placed one of the best winning penalties you are likely to see into the top left-hand corner. Solo had no chance, as the sound of the ball hitting the net was heard by forty-eight thousand people in the stadium, and fifteen million Japanese fans watching at home.

Japan had succeeded where China had failed in 1999 – they had beaten the United States on penalties, and won Asia its first senior World Cup, this, just four months after the country was crippled by the tragedy of the tsunami.

'It meant a lot to me personally,' said Kumagai.

'I was transferring to Frankfurt after the World Cup and becoming a world champion helped to make me known to people in Germany. This whole journey to the championship definitely led to my personal growth. Also, I was very glad that we were able to give girls in Asia a dream.

'There really were a lot of people who said to us thank you for the impressive performance and courage. I think we cheered people up in Japan through our football and I was glad that we managed to bring good news back when Japan was going through the aftermath of the disaster.'

The team, aware of the support and warmth they had received from nations around the world during the tournament, displayed a banner that read: 'To our friends around the world. Thank you for your support.'

Homare Sawa, who lofted the World Cup trophy above her head, was named the Player of the Tournament, and six months later would be recognised as the best women's footballer in the world as she collected the FIFA Women's Player of the Year for 2011.

Abby Wambach, who finished third in the scoring charts at the tournament and was named as part of the competition's All-Star team, reflected on the defeat, looking at it from both sides of the coin. She admitted that at the time, there were mixed feelings about the final loss. On the one hand, Japan had been through so much and a victory like this brought some form of joy and celebration. But as a competitor, there was a feeling of disappointment, disappointment from a personal level, and from a team perspective:

'As a competitor, I wanted to win, obviously, and I think, outwardly, the things that I was saying, I kind of half-believed, because of course their country went through a really traumatic experience with the tsunami. I could see a sane part of myself feeling grateful for them and happy for them.

'But I also, as a competitor, committed all of myself to winning that tournament. And knowing that, that team changed the course – in a lot of ways – of my personal experience . . . I was probably going to be given the Golden Ball, and then Sawa steps in and scores this ridiculous volley with the outside of her foot, with her eyes closed – literally – and then she gets pushed into the position of best player of the tournament and player of the year. I don't even care about personal awards, but the competitor inside of me wants to make sure that our team is on the winning side of all competitions that we go into.

'I was heartbroken, and it took me a long time to understand why those circumstances ended up the way that they did. And the truth of that matter is that nobody knows. Japan was meant to win that game. We hit the post in the first half and Lauren Cheney, Megan Rapinoe, they got into a position where I thought that we probably should have been up by two or maybe even three by half-time. And that just wasn't the case. Our team had something more to learn, and I think that's what the next four years, leading into the 2015 World Cup, was trying to figure out what we needed to learn to get the result that we wanted.

'But of course, as a competitor I can't lie and say that the better team won. I actually don't believe that Japan was the better team that day; I just feel like sometimes finals, because they are heightened and because they are more emotional, the results are not always in favour of the best team. But I do recognise that Japan was the better team that day because they were lifting the trophy at the end of the tournament. It was a huge win for their country, so I understand both sides of that coin.'

It would be hard to begrudge Japan's victory having gone through so much and overcome the odds to claim a World Cup. Praise was heaped on them from around the world, with congratulatory messages coming from some of the most well-recognised public figures.

United States President Barack Obama tweeted his congratulations having watched the match with his family, while Junji Ogura, president of the Japanese football association, highlighted that this was more than just about football:

'The players have showed the brilliance of Japanese women.'

Japan hadn't only won a World Cup, they had won the hearts of the world that was watching. They had brought joy to a nation that four months earlier was in search of the slightest bit of hope.

It's moments like this which make the World Cup so special.

Acknowledgements

....

Thank you to everyone who helped make this book possible: Kelly Smith, Anna Kessel, Julie Foudy, Abby Wambach, Ariane Hingst, Steph Houghton, Leslie Osborne, April Heinrichs, Carin Gabarra, Lisa De Vanna, Caitlin Foord, Aaron Heifetz, Ben O'Neill, Rainer Hennies, Nadine Angerer, Emily Liles, Tony Leighton, Matthew Buck, Kay Cossington, Carla Overbeck, Anson Dorrance, Heather O'Reilly, Megan Rapinoe, Alicia Ferguson, Anthony DiCicco, Elise Kellond-Knight, Alen Stajcic, Jess Fishlock, Saki Kumagai, Carli Lloyd, James Galanis, Ann Odong, Tom Sermanni, Hampton Dellinger, Rocky Collis and Ayako Tanaka.

And to the team at Robinson, for believing in the need for this book.

Index